To Jeff;

On the start of

your 401(k) C

All the Best,

[signature]

Jan. 2012

D0397560

Fund Spy

Fund Spy

Morningstar's Inside Secrets to Selecting Mutual Funds That Outperform

Russel Kinnel

WILEY

John Wiley & Sons, Inc.

Published by John Wiley & Sons, Inc., Hoboken, New Jersey.

Published simultaneously in Canada.

For general information on our other products and services or for technical support, please contact our Customer Care Department within the United States at (800) 762-2974, outside the United States at (317) 572-3993 or fax (317) 572-4002.

Wiley also publishes its books in a variety of electronic formats. Some content that appears in print may not be available in electronic books. For more information about Wiley products, visit our Web site at www.wiley.com.

ISBN-13 978-0-470-41401-9

Printed in the United States of America

10 9 8 7 6 5 4 3 2 1

For Elisabeth

Contents

Foreword

MANY MUTUAL FUND GUIDES, quite frankly, are tired rehashings of stale academic papers. They run you through the history and evolution of the fund industry and discuss the efficient frontier, the importance of diversification, and the necessity of a long-term perspective, but they always pull back when it gets to the good stuff, the stuff that really matters—whom you can trust and why. That's certainly not the case with *Fund Spy*, a book built entirely around original research, as well as pull-no-punches opinions on how you should invest and to whom you can entrust your savings. This book is the real deal, an insider's guide to what the fund industry is like—the good, the bad, and the funny.

Mutual fund analysis is at the very core of Morningstar's identity, and while there are many teams of great people at the company, there's no group more passionate in their mission than Morningstar's fund analysts. I ought to know. I was the company's first analyst, and it has been a delight to see the team evolve over the past two decades. Crucial to the team's growth has been the immense contribution of Russ Kinnel. As you'll see in the pages that follow, Russ brings keen insights, a wicked wit, and a genuine concern for the small investor to his work. He's a wonderful writer and has led many groundbreaking research efforts, several of which are detailed here. Moreover, he's a blast to work with. No one sends a sharper, funnier e-mail than Russ.

Fund Spy gives a great picture of what it's like to be a fund analyst at Morningstar. Trading costs, managers investing (or not) in their own funds, variations on an investment style—these are the kinds of things we discuss daily and work to teach our new analysts about. Russ has condensed 20 years of our collective learning into a tidy primer that would be a great asset for any fund investor. He doesn't kowtow to fund industry interests; he simply does what we ask all our analysts to do: Tell the story as fairly and accurately as possible, and do it from the investor's perspective. When you can do all that and combine it with Russ's wit, you've got a winning combination.

In the pages that follow, you'll get the inside dope on how to assess a fund manager's commitment, why costs matter so much to your results, and how to avoid common pitfalls in fund selection and portfolio construction. But like any great storyteller, Russ saves the best for last. His rundown on the top fund shops—both load and no-load—and his take on the best, time-tested funds are both dead on the mark. I wouldn't change a word. Having Russ at your side when navigating the world of mutual funds is like having Quentin Tarantino helping you fill your Netflix list, or having Lester Bangs at your side as you sort through stacks of classic rock and roll records. Even if you know the territory, you're sure to learn something new and discover some hidden gems.

Enjoy!

DON PHILLIPS
Managing Director
Morningstar

Preface

I STARTED AT Morningstar in 1994. That year, interest rates were spiking, and the Mexican equity bubble inspired by NAFTA turned into a panic. Soon after that, California's Orange County defaulted on a slew of debt brought on by unwise mortgage investments. Over the ensuing years, we saw a Russian default mess, an Asian meltdown, the bailout of Long-Term Capital Management, the bursting of the Internet bubble, the attacks of September 11, wars in Iraq and Afghanistan, the corporate meltdowns of Enron and WorldCom, and, most recently, the subprime housing bubble bursting and shaking financial institutions to their knees.

Yet somehow, we got the largest bull market in there somewhere, and nearly all the top money managers and investment firms are still standing with strong long-term results to show for it. Yes, buy-and-hold investing still works, while trendier strategies have their moments and then collapse. With the markets at depressed levels (as of fourth quarter 2008), this is a great time to invest with good managers, provided you're in it for the long term.

I started writing Morningstar's Fund Spy column back in 1997, and over the years I've shared lots of ideas, observations, and laughs at the fund world's occasionally out-of-control marketing departments. I'll share the results of years of research and a lot of experience from talking with managers and seeing the difference between words and deeds.

My aim is to make investing much easier for you by showing you the key data points and sharing my years of research on the best managers. You don't need a ton of data or sophisticated programs—just focus and patience. I'll show you the handful of quantitative and qualitative factors you need to pick winning funds. In fact, I've built it all into an easy-to-use tool at www.morningstar.com/goto/Fundspy. Just plug in a fund ticker or name and you're good to go.

If recent markets have you jaded and you think all mutual funds are the same, take another look. In Chapter 1, I'll reveal the huge gap between the returns of above-average and below-average funds. You'll see that it will be a lot easier to reach your long-term goals if most of your funds outperform.

We've long known that low costs and dedication to clients were the keys to successful funds, but now we have some new tools to do a better job of finding funds that meet those criteria. We now have data on how much fund managers are investing in their funds so that we can more accurately judge their commitment to shareholders. In Chapter 2, I'll look at how to separate the good managers from the indifferent.

In Chapter 3, I'll shine a light on a crucial piece of information that has been hidden all these years: trading costs. Trading costs are as big and important as expense ratios, but until we came out with our data on trading costs, individual investors had no way of knowing what they were. I'll show you how we calculate trading costs, what they mean, and how they will help you to improve your fund selection.

The other half of the cost equation is expense ratios. If you're skeptical about the importance of expenses, allow me to show you that they're more important than you think. In Chapter 4, I'll show you that fund companies hide a lot of their high-cost losers in a way that obscures the awful truth about fund costs. More importantly, I'll show you just how much you can improve your chances of success with low-cost funds.

But what about performance? I'm glad you asked, because I'll show you how to avoid the performance trap of betting the ranch on tempting recent results. There's a better way to use returns; I'll walk you through it in Chapter 5.

The importance of quantitative factors in choosing the right funds is huge, but so is the qualitative side. For starters you need to understand fund strategies and the risk they entail in order to build a sound portfolio and to use funds wisely. I'll make it easy for you in Chapter 6. We see lots of good funds that investors end up using poorly because they didn't contemplate the downside inherent in a fund's strategy. This bit isn't part of the formula, but it should be part of your process because you have to know what you own.

You are essentially hiring a manager or managers to handle your life savings, so you need to know how to pick good managers and avoid the ones that let conflicts of interest get the better of them. In Chapter 7, I'll help you to spot the good ones and introduce you to our stewardship grades. At Morningstar, we have years of experience interviewing managers and evaluating funds, and we also sift through all the SEC filings and do on-site visits to find out which firms really care about shareholders. We boil all that down to a letter grade.

In Chapters 8 and 9, I'll provide you a nice and easy cheat sheet to make the most of different fund companies. Even if you had access to the managers and analysts, you probably don't have the time to meet with them, make follow-up phone calls, and do all the work that is necessary to fully understand a fund company. That's why I share my insight from 14 years of research, as well as all the visits and calls our outstanding fund analyst staff has done. Where should you go for index funds or momentum funds, for example? I'll tell you. Chapter 8 is for do-it-yourself investors in no-load funds and Chapter 9 is for those who buy through a full-service broker.

Finally, in Chapter 10, I'll share 20 funds that aced all the tests laid out in the book. I'll even tell you what each fund's competitive edge is and which red flags to watch out for so you'll know when to sell.

Acknowledgments

GREGG WOLPER, KAREN DOLAN, KAREN WALLACE, AND HAYWOOD KELLY edited this book and were a tremendous help to me. Maureen Dahlen's work as business and project manager was invaluable.

The groundwork for much of Morningstar's research over the years including this book was laid by CEO Joe Mansueto; president of Individual Investor Business Unit Catherine Gillis Odelbo; managing director Don Phillips; vice president of research John Rekenthaler; and director of research Paul Kaplan in our central research group.

Many of the studies appearing here or influencing work here were run by Annette Larson and Mark Komissorauk. In addition, Bridget Bulger and Kailin Liu helped with all manner of research tasks.

Kunal Kapoor and Christopher Traulsen developed our stewardship grade methodology, and Laura Pavlenko Lutton refined it.

Our trading cost work built on a paper by Roger Edelen, Greg Kadlec, and Richard Evans.

In addition, all of my work has been informed by our Director of Personal Finance Christine Benz and our outstanding fund analyst staff headed by Karen Dolan. The senior analysts are Michael Breen, Dan Culloton, Arijit Dutta, Andrew Gogerty, Bridget Hughes, Eric Jacobson, Lawrence Jones, Laura Pavlenko Lutton, William Samuel Rocco, and Gregg Wolper. I'm also indebted to all the former fund analysts at Morningstar who have contributed so much to our knowledge of funds as well as the thousands of mutual fund managers who have taken the time to talk with us over the years, and the subscribers to our publications who have engaged us in an enlightening dialogue and provided remarkable support through bear markets and bull markets alike.

The Remarkable Gap Between Winners and Losers

THIS BOOK IS ALL ABOUT picking winning funds, so let's take a look at what you'll win if you select good funds.

Too often, people assume that one fund is as good as the next. Or they put in the effort to pick their stock funds but buy their bond funds from whichever fund company is most convenient. But that's leaving a lot of money on the table.

As the immortal Spinal Tap lead singer David St. Hubbins said, "It's such a fine line between stupid, and clever." Put a little time into your fund selection, and you'll be on the right side of the St. Hubbins line.

It's amazing to me how people will spend way more time researching fun expenditures, like cars and plasma TVs, than they will on developing an investment plan and selecting their investments. Sure, it isn't as fun, but it's your retirement, your house, and your kids' college education!

Let's look at why it's worth a little effort. It's not too hard to pick funds that will do a little better than average, and it takes only a little more work to upgrade from there so that you've meaningfully improved your chances of returns that are well above average while reducing your chances of lousy performance. Of course, there's no foolproof method of predicting the top-performing fund over the next 10 years, but there are dependable methods to select funds that should earn strong returns while limiting cellar-dwellers.

The Forest for the Trees

Sometimes short-term returns, such as those for a six-month period, can be all bunched together. From that perspective, funds in a particular category might all look alike. If you step back and look at the effects of long-term compounding, however, the differences get dramatic. You can see the gaps in Figure 1.1, where even among low-returning bond funds the gap is quite wide.

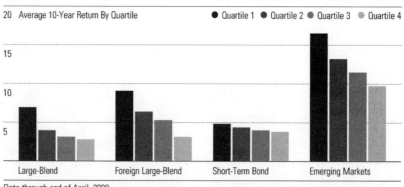

Data through end of April, 2008.

You don't have to pick the best fund. Just pick a good one and you'll make thousands more than you would have in a weak performer.

Figure 1.1   The Enormous Gap Between Winning and Losing Funds
Source: Morningstar

Let's consider the returns of large-blend funds returns over the past 10 years. The large-blend category, which is home to a passel of S&P 500 Index funds, might seem like a bunch of bland benchmark-huggers. But consider the differences in average 10-year annualized returns for each quartile through April 2008: Funds in the top quartile gained 7.02 percent per year over the 10-year period; funds in the second quartile rose 4.06 percent per year; the third, 3.23 percent; and the fourth, 2.9 percent. That's a huge gap from the top quartile to the second and down to the fourth. In honor of St. Hubbins, let's call the gap between the top and bottom quartiles the *stupid penalty*. In the case of large-blend funds, it's more than 400 basis points. Put in dollar terms, $100,000 invested 10 years ago in the typical top-quartile large-blend fund grew to $197,000 today, versus

Top 10 Best Things About Mutual Funds

1. Diversification is better than you get on your own.

2. There is greater transparency than any other managed account.

3. They bring great management to individual investors.

4. Low-cost funds are the best deal in investing.

5. They enable you to invest outside your area of expertise.

6. They are easy to compare.

7. Audited portfolios make theft nearly impossible.

8. You can get in or out every day at net asset value.

9. Some have track records that are decades long.

10. You can invest automatically without paying commissions.

$149,000 for the second quartile and $133,000 for the worst—making a stupid penalty of $64,000!

The gap remains dramatic in other categories. For the foreign-large-blend group, the top quartile returned 9.16 percent, compared with 6.49 percent, 5.38 percent, and 3.24 percent for the three other quartiles, respectively. For the intermediate-bond fund category, returns were 6.02 percent, 5.25 percent, 4.85 percent, and 4.07 percent. That's a big gap for high-quality bond funds. Then, I checked two categories at the extreme ends of the risk spectrum and found not much changed in the gaps. For short-term bond funds, the breakdown was 4.93 percent, 4.47 percent, 4.10 percent, and 3.91 percent. It's amazing to think that you can do 100 basis points better per year in a category where yields and returns are so tightly bunched. For the diversified-emerging-markets-stock category, returns were 16.62 percent, 13.31 percent, 11.58 percent, and 9.84 percent.

One of the most striking aspects of the study is that it even works across categories. Except for the emerging-markets-stock fund category, you could take the top quartile of one of the four other categories and beat the bottom quartile of other groups. For example, you'd have been better off in a top-quartile short-term-bond fund than a bottom-quartile or even second-best-quartile large-blend fund. The top quartile of intermediate-bond funds beat the bottom-half returns for the foreign-large-blend group.

Improve Your Chances of Success

In short, you'll make it much easier to beat your investment goals if you can select outperformers. This book will show you how to do that. No, you won't bat 1.000, but you should be able to be on the right side of the St. Hubbins line most of the time.

Don't settle for high-cost, poorly run funds simply because they fell into your portfolio or someone is touting them. Take the time to research and buy funds that will work for the long haul. Three months or even a year from now, you may not see a difference, but you will see a dramatic difference in 10 and 20 years, when the power of compounding has grown your portfolio.

The returns we just reviewed include only funds that were good enough to survive in the first place. It's tough to take into account those funds that were around for only part of the time period. Suffice it to say that if we could factor those in, the gap would be even greater. The crummiest funds are the ones generally killed off, so the bottom-quartile figures would be even worse if extinct funds could be included.

Welcome to Lake Wobegon

Lest you think that finding better funds is a daunting task, consider this: The average fund investor actually does better than the average fund, despite making key errors. Yes, that sounds like Lake Wobegon where everyone is above average, but it's just a matter of two different averages. It does seem hard to believe, considering that many fund investors are lousy timers. They buy hot sectors after they have gone up a lot, and they panic and sell poor-performing sectors just before they rally. Yet they actually compensate for their bad timing by picking above-average funds.

In 2006, I used asset-weighting to find out how the typical investor did. That means I weighted fund returns based on asset size at the end of each month. When you do that, you see that investors typically fare worse than the actual stated returns for a fund because of lousy timing of purchases and sales. In fact, I first wrote about this in a *Morningstar Fund-Investor* commentary titled "Mind the Gap" published in 2005. Financial pundits ate this up with a spoon because it made fund companies and fund investors look bad, and justifiably so.

But in a 2006 study, I took the extra step of asset-weighting those investor returns so that I could see how the average investor did overall. It turns out that collectively, fund investors actually did better than the average category performance because they chose better-than-average funds (see Figure 1.2).

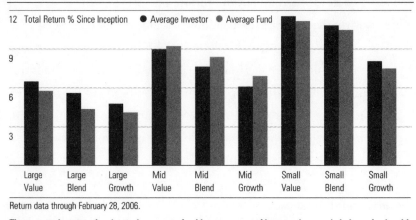

| 12 Total Return % Since Inception | ● Average Investor | ● Average Fund |

Return data through February 28, 2006.

The average investor often beats the average fund because most of investors' money is in large funds with below average costs.

Figure 1.2   The Average Investor versus the Average Fund

Interestingly, none of the pundits picked up this follow-up story. In fact, the earlier study is still cited far more than the latter because financial writers like the elitist sound of it. Fund companies and fund investors are idiots—end of story. The follow-up study shows that the average investor isn't quite that much of a dolt, but that won't sell newspapers or really high-priced hedge funds.

Why does the average investor beat the average fund? The main reason is costs. Big funds generally have lower costs because the funds pass along some economies of scale to fundholders. (Don't worry—they keep plenty for themselves.) In fact, the difference between the average fund investor's performance and the average fund's performance is almost exactly the same as the difference between the asset-weighted expense ratio and the average expense ratio.

Fund investors and their advisors find their way to bigger, lower-cost funds for a wide range of reasons. Some seek out lower costs; others like to consolidate their accounts, and the big fund companies (which tend to have cheaper funds) make that easy. Others go through brokerages, which favor certain big fund companies, and some just buy them because they're in their 401(k). In addition, there's a self-reinforcing aspect to this, as lower-cost funds tend to outperform, thereby attracting assets, and that, in turn, lowers the expense ratio further.

FAQs

Q. When you say better than average, what group are you averaging?

A. I'm referring to the average return of a fund category. Categories are our way of classifying funds. Comparing returns within a category enables you to assess a fund's performance. The categories are also helpful in building a diversified portfolio. We base the categories on three years' worth of portfolio data. For example, we group domestic stock funds by our Style Box with categories such as small value and mid-growth.

Q. What is the Morningstar Style Box™?

A. The Style Box is a nine-box grid we use to analyze funds; the categories are based on them. We've found that funds with similar market cap, value, and growth characteristics tend to behave in similar fashion and invest in similar holdings. It's divided by market cap vertically (small, mid, and large) and value/growth horizontally (value, blend, and growth). We use five value characteristics and five growth characteristics to determine where a fund plots on the y axis.

Conclusion

So, if the typical investor can easily find his way to an above-average fund, imagine what you can do when you intelligently target the key factors that drive fund performance. Only a few investors are using all of the tools I'm going to share with you in this book. Some are brand new, and others are tried and true.

Armed with the right strategy, you can do better than the average fund *and* the average investor. With better information, you can avoid the timing mistakes that so many investors make, and you'll be well on your way to reaching your goals.

2

Does Your Manager Eat His Own Cooking?

IF I ASKED you if the managers of your mutual funds invested in their funds, your first reaction might be, "Of course they do." It turns out that most don't.

Some managers really do mean it when they say they consider fund-holders partners, while others don't. Until recently, everyone could talk big, but then the SEC started requiring managers to actually disclose their investments.

The good news is that hundreds of managers have more than $1 million of their own money in the funds. The bad news is that thousands don't have a dime in their funds. Apparently, those fund ads and slick brokers' pitches didn't even convince the folks running the fund to invest.

Let's take a look at the gory details.

How Ownership Is Disclosed

The disclosure rules say that managers must disclose ownership in the following ranges:

- ▶ $0
- ▶ $1–$10,000
- ▶ $10,001–$50,000
- ▶ $50,001–$100,000
- ▶ $100,001–$500,000
- ▶ $500,001–$1 million
- ▶ Over $1 million

Each manager on a fund must disclose his or her investment.

The ownership figures are disclosed in the Statement of Additional Information (SAI), which is a companion document to the prospectus. Not many people read their funds' prospectuses, let alone go to the trouble of asking the fund company to send the SAI, too. You can go the fund company's Web site or the SEC's Edgar site (www.sec.gov/edgar.shtml) to try and track the SAI down and then search the SAI on the manager's name to see if you can find the ownership information.

However, to make it a lot easier (much to the annoyance of managers who don't invest in their funds), Morningstar's data group has gathered the data on all mutual funds. You can find the information in our fund data pages on Morningstar.com, and you can also find it by plugging in the ticker of a fund on the special Web site for this book: www.morningstar.com/goto/fundspy.

Managers Hate Their Own Cooking

The figures that jump off the page are those where no manager invested a dime. In U.S.-stock funds, 46 percent report no manager ownership. And it gets worse from there. Fully 59 percent of foreign-stock funds have no ownership (though some had a reasonable excuse), 65 percent of taxable-bond funds have no ownership, 70 percent of balanced funds put up goose eggs, and 78 percent of muni funds lack ownership.

There are really only two legitimate reasons for not owning a fund you run. First, if you run a single-state municipal-bond fund for a state other than the one you live in, it doesn't make sense to own that fund, as you won't benefit from the tax breaks. Second, managers who are citizens of foreign countries have a good excuse if their country bars investment in U.S.-domiciled funds. Foreign citizens run a number of foreign-stock funds, and that may account for the ownership difference between U.S.-stock funds and international-stock funds. For managers who run niche funds or run a lot of funds, there's good reason for them to be at the lower end of the ranges, but not at zero.

The number of managers who don't eat their own cooking is staggering. With the two exceptions I spelled out, I can't think of why anyone should invest in a fund that its own manager doesn't invest in. True, higher investment levels aren't a guarantee of success or an ethical manager, but at least they show that managers believe in the funds and they are willing to pay the same costs and taxes that the rest of shareholders do.

So, for a core fund, demand manager investment in the top two levels ($500,000 or higher). For niche funds, any amount greater than $100,000 is okay.

Top 10 Worst Things About Mutual Funds

1. Capital gains are taxed as the fund realizes them rather than when you sell.

2. Assets can grow so large that they hurt performance.

3. There is too much manager turnover.

(Continued)

4. Too many funds have high portfolio turnover.

5. Fund supermarkets jack up fees.

6. Funds run meaningless ads.

7. Bad records can be hidden.

8. Huge fund complexes sometimes have more funds than good managers.

9. 12b-1 fees.

10. Inflows and outflows complicate a manager's job and hurt returns.

Looking at Investment Levels at Our Recommended Funds

To take another angle on it, let's examine how managers of funds on our recommended list and our sell list stack up on manager investment.

It turns out that we're not the only ones who have more conviction in our Fund Analyst Picks than our Fund Analyst Pans. Assuming the midpoint of each range, we found an average investment of $370,000 for our Fund Analyst Picks compared with $54,000 for our average pan.

That's a factor of nearly 7.

If we exclude areas where managers have reasonable excuses, such as target-date, single-state muni, and index funds, the average pick's investment pops up to $503,000. That illustrates the conviction we look for, as well as the alignment of interests with shareholders'.

Is it an accident that managers are reluctant to invest in the pans, which suffer from some combination of high costs, poor strategy, shaky management, and disappointing stewardship? The median pick has about $240,000 invested by each manager. Conversely, the median pan has $0 invested.

Twenty-seven of our picks could claim that all of their managers have at least $1 million invested, and 55 have at least one manager with more than $1 million.

How Do Fund Companies Shake Out?

So, how much do managers across different fund companies invest? It turns out that there's a huge difference among fund companies and that tells you a lot about the partners'/rubes' side of the equation. I broke out manager investment by asset class for the 30 largest fund companies.

As you can see in Table 2.1, the top boutique-type firms rate best, whereas some of the big broker-sold companies are at the bottom. It's no accident that the firms with the highest manager investment have longer tenures, better performance, and lower fees than those at the bottom, where the firm may consider a strong sales force more important than a strong management team.

FAQs

Q. If I'm looking for a single-state muni fund where the manager might have reason not to invest, is there some way I can use manager investment levels to pick the right fund?

A. Yes, you can look at the manager's investment levels in other funds to see if the manager at least buys into his or her process. In addition, some fund companies disclose managers' investments throughout the fund company.

Q. How often is the information updated?

A. It's updated yearly, though some fund companies update it twice a year. That's worth keeping in mind regarding a new manager at a fund where the first filing might actually cover a period before he or she started at the fund.

Table 2.1 Average Manager Ownership at the Largest Fund Companies

Family	Average Median Ownership	% of Managers with Median Ownership $1Mil or More	$0
First Eagle	1,000,000	100.00	0.00
Oakmark	1,000,000	100.00	0.00
Dodge & Cox	664,773	47.73	0.00
Davis Funds	499,412	35.29	0.00
American Funds	456,622	27.66	6.38
T. Rowe Price	244,670	10.38	38.68
Janus	231,856	17.53	67.01
Thornburg	203,000	13.33	46.67
Putnam	177,467	6.00	41.33
Lord Abbett	159,048	9.52	32.38
Fidelity Investments	149,875	8.41	55.14
Vanguard	147,985	8.74	72.33
MFS	145,950	4.13	46.28
Morgan Stanley	135,457	7.31	60.27
Pioneer Investments	135,402	4.60	49.43
Invesco Aim	125,461	3.29	54.61
JennisonDryden	105,071	4.29	67.14
Evergreen	104,494	1.27	30.38
Van Kampen	101,014	2.90	64.49
Harbor	91,852	7.41	77.78
Franklin Templeton Investments	88,985	1.92	60.92
Eaton Vance	88,924	3.16	73.42
Wells Fargo Advantage	86,563	3.37	65.87
Columbia	82,239	2.61	65.65
American Century Investments	80,090	1.79	59.64
Hartford Mutual Funds	78,761	2.56	67.52
AllianceBernstein	66,447	4.74	84.74
RiverSource	65,859	0.52	62.50
BlackRock	65,830	3.14	79.82
GMO	56,146	4.17	83.33
Goldman Sachs	52,712	0.42	71.19
JP Morgan	52,701	1.92	67.43
USAA	49,947	2.11	82.11
OppenheimerFunds	47,939	0.88	78.51
PIMCO Funds	46,140	3.51	91.23
Federated	35,174	0.87	85.22
Legg Mason Partners	30,648	1.04	91.19
DWS Investments	22,050	0.84	72.80
John Hancock	17,326	0.00	90.00
Schwab Funds	15,385	0.00	78.46

Source: Morningstar Inc. Data as of October 1, 2008.

Q. Would an investor be able to determine by looking at the SAI whether a manager invests in a separate account or overseas fund similar to the U.S. mutual fund?

A. Not in the SEC filings; they cover only that specific fund.

Q. Can you find out if a fund's directors invest in the fund?

A. Yes; mutual fund directors have to report their ownership, though remarkably, the top of the range is only $100,000.

Conclusion

Manager investments are one of those spots in the fund world where the velvet curtain is pulled back and you get a glimpse of what's really going on. Are things as they say, or is it just a bunch of marketing? The fund company data reveal that there are big differences in commitments to fund shareholders among the fund companies.

No fund manager would touch a company where the CEO didn't own stock, and I wouldn't buy a fund where the manager didn't invest. The more the fund manager has invested, the better his or her incentives are aligned with shareholders'. It doesn't guarantee that the manager will do a brilliant job, but it does weed out those managers who don't believe in their process or fee structure or haven't invested because they are about to leave for a more lucrative offer.

3

New Trading Cost Estimates Shed Light on a Big Mystery

TRADING COSTS ARE important. We've known that for a long time. But mutual funds don't have to tell you what they are, so there wasn't much you could do about it. Most fund investors don't know what trading costs are, let alone how much they hurt performance.

Say you own $100,000 of a momentum fund. Its expense ratio might be costing you $1,000 a year. But trading costs, which aren't reported but nevertheless eat into the value of your account, could total $2,500 every year!

In 1994, Jack Bogle argued that invisible trading costs were probably as great as expense ratios and just as damaging to total returns. Expense ratios are the most powerful predictor of future fund performance, so a second measure of equal power would be quite valuable. Since Bogle's hypothesis, the hunt for the fund world's "dark matter" has been on.

Unfortunately, the starting point for fund investors is a pretty crummy one. Turnover is the closest publicly disclosed figure to trading costs. However, it's so flawed that it isn't much help. Turnover is the lesser of purchases or sales made by the fund divided by assets. By taking the lesser rather than the average or sum, the SEC helps the fund industry understate how much it is trading.

Turnover is especially misleading when huge sums of outflows or inflows might well lead a fund to make almost all of its trades on one side of the ledger. Say the fund bought $100 million in stock but sold only $1 million and it has $100 million in assets. Then, its official turnover would be 1 percent—vastly understating the amount of trades.

Academics and Morningstar have tested turnover to see if it predicts mutual fund returns and found it is of little help. Even if turnover were calculated correctly, it would still leave you well short of trading costs. Let's take a look at what goes into trading costs to understand why, and then I'll walk you through our big breakthrough on the subject. And be sure to check out your fund's costs at www.morningstar.com/goto/fundspy.

What Are Trading Costs?

When you or I trade stocks, we think of the commission as the trading cost. But for a mutual fund, that's a tiny portion of true trading cost. Big stock trades actually move stock prices. There are many components of trading costs:

▶ **Brokerage costs**. This is the obvious bit. Typically, funds pay commissions of between one and five cents per share on a stock, which is generally a better price than a typical investor would get trading 100 shares of a stock, though sometimes those costs include soft dollar purchases of research and are higher than the rock-bottom price. The bigger fund companies can drive a harder bargain on them.

▶ **Market impact**. You can trade 1,000 shares of General Electric all day and not push the stock price around, but if you trade 1 million shares, you will push the price higher when you buy and down when you sell. Say it's trading at $40, and by the time you finish it's at $44, your average price on the stock is $42, and you paid 3 cents a share in commissions. Now, your price impact is $2/share and your commission is 3 cents/share. When you go to sell, you'll push the price down by $2 a share again and pay 3 cents/share. All told, your cost is $4.06 per share on that trade. That means you better be right about GE, because it has to outperform the stock you sold to buy it by that trading cost just to break even. The effect is magnified many times over for smaller stocks that are less heavily traded.

▶ **Momentum**. A fund isn't trading in a vacuum, and the stock price could move for reasons unrelated to the fund's trade. The same thing that spurred the fund to buy GE could have led others to do the same, running the stock price up. Then the manager has the unpleasant decision of either paying a higher price or accepting a smaller position in GE. Either one is a cost that hurts the fund's returns. In addition, word could leak out about the trade, or others might figure it out from available data on trades and ownership and start making their own trades ahead of you and drive your prices up even more. Prices can even move away from the price a manager wants because of delays in the process of making the trade.

▶ **Bid/ask spreads**. A fund, particularly one investing overseas, might pay a steep cost on each trade due to wide spreads between the bid and ask price—a hidden commission for brokers and market makers.

▶ **Flow-driven costs—a.k.a. the price of convenience**. Money flowing in and out of funds hurts performance by causing unnecessary trades.

People love the convenience of being able to buy or sell a mutual fund any day they want to. But it comes at a cost. Having lots of money sloshing in and out means a fund manager has to invest when he doesn't have an information edge. A fund's strategy is about exploiting some research advantage that uncovers values or problems not priced into the stock. But if money comes into the fund on a day when the manager wouldn't otherwise be buying, the manager still has to put that money to work or let it sit on the sidelines and dilute returns in a rally. It turns out that those flow-driven trades are much less likely to be profitable than strategy-driven trades, according to studies done by Roger Edelen, Greg Kadlec, and Richard Evans. ("Scale effects in mutual fund performance: The role of trading costs," March 17, 2007)

Top 10 Funds to Recommend to Your Relatives
1. Vanguard STAR (VGSTX)
2. Dodge & Cox Balanced (DODBX)
3. T. Rowe Price Target-Date Funds
4. Fidelity Spartan Total Market (FSTMX)
5. American Funds EuroPacific Growth (AEPGX)
6. Vanguard Target-Date Funds
7. American Funds Washington Mutual (AWSHX)
8. Harbor Bond (HABDX)
9. T. Rowe Price Equity Income (PRFDX)
10. Vanguard Intermediate-Term Tax Exempt (VWITX)

Dark Matter Revealed

Over the years, fund companies, consultants, traders, and academics have learned quite a lot about trading costs, mainly by examining actual trades at fund companies. None are in complete agreement about how to calculate costs, but there is a growing consensus about the basics.

The tricky part for us, though, is that fund companies don't disclose their estimates or their trades. That means we have to figure out trading costs from publicly available information. It's a tough nut to crack, but the analysts at Morningstar have put together data on fund portfolios with the trading expertise of Reflow Inc. and the academic rigor of trading experts Edelen, Kadlec, and Evans.

Employing trading cost estimates in your fund selection process can provide a real boost to your returns. In Figure 3.1, I pinched a table from a paper published by Edelen, Kadlec, and Evans that shows how much performance degrades with high trading costs. They used alpha—a measure of how much value is added by a manager versus the fund benchmark—to test the impact. You can see that the highest trading cost quintile performed far worse than those with lower trading costs. On the right side, it shows the corrosive effects of expense ratios for comparison purposes.

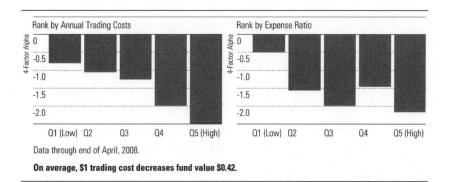

Rank by Annual Trading Costs

Rank by Expense Ratio

Data through end of April, 2008.

On average, $1 trading cost decreases fund value $0.42.

Figure 3.1   How Trading Costs and Expense Ratios Erode Funds

How to Do It

The key drivers in trading cost estimates are trade size, market capitalization, and momentum. I've illustrated the trade size issue already, so let's skip ahead to market cap. Smaller stocks trade less frequently and have greater bid/ask spreads than large caps. That means they cost more to trade—especially in the case of large orders.

Momentum is another word for hot stocks. When a company is on a roll and everyone wants to get in, purchases drive up the prices much faster than normal. Thus, momentum strategies incur greater trading costs than those more contrarian strategies that involve buying the stocks that everyone is desperate to sell.

Step 1. Look at the amount and size of trades across similar funds and rank order the funds from highest to lowest.

Step 2. Control for momentum, market cap, and style.

Step 3. Figure out the actual cost by examining past performance of the different groups, ranked by trading costs. We see how much returns were hurt by the different groups and can then figure a marginal cost of trading based on the slope of the line.

Putting It to Use

As with expense ratios, you can screen out funds with high trading cost and home in on funds with high probabilities of success. At a minimum, throw out those with above-average trading costs for their category.

You could also sum up expense ratios and trading costs, then throw out those with above-average costs. And when making the final cut, take a look at your finalists' total costs and pick the one with lower costs.

For funds you already own, watch out for a spike in trading costs. It could mean that the fund has taken in too much new money and that is what is driving up trading costs. When a fund grows, it has to make bigger trades. That's not a problem until it reaches a tipping point when its market impact starts to soar. Then, you should consider moving on.

Because market capitalization is a key piece of the puzzle, be sure to take a close look at your small-cap funds' trading costs. Low-turnover large-cap funds are less likely to be a problem.

Trading costs are not really a problem for high-quality bond funds. Junk bonds are less liquid and tend to trade on company specifics more like stocks, so it's possible trading costs are important for high-yield funds.

FAQs

Q. Do index funds have trading costs?

A. Yes; those that track higher-turnover indexes will incur costs. However, we can see that index funds tracking the S&P 500 and Wilshire 5000 generally lag their index by just the expense ratio. That implies that they have no trading costs.

Q. Is it possible for funds to make a trading profit?

A. Yes; we can't capture it because we don't see actual trades, but a fund that acts as a provider of liquidity can make a profit. That means that rather than targeting a specific stock, they look to capture the bid/ask spread by buying when sellers are eager to get out or selling when buyers are desperate to buy. Trading consultants say there are funds with positive trading costs over 100 basis points.

Q. Do foreign funds have higher trading costs?

A. Yes, it costs more to trade overseas—particularly in emerging markets.

Q. Are taxes included in trading costs?

A. No. We calculate a tax cost ratio in order to estimate a fund's tax bill.

Q. Why doesn't the SEC require funds to disclose trading costs?

A. The first reason is that there are different views of how to calculate trading costs so it's hard to reach consensus on the right methodology. The second reason is that the fund industry doesn't want to reach consensus because that could lead to disclosure of trading costs—they'd rather keep them under the rug.

Q. Do fund managers know what their trading costs are?

A. Some get detailed reports and understand the trade-offs involved. Others are blissfully ignorant.

Q. Will trading costs gain widespread use in selecting funds?

A. I expect savvy fund investors, consultants, and high-end financial planners to incorporate this data quickly, but the average investors and their brokers will still be more dazzled by last year's returns.

Conclusion

Trading cost estimates will make it much easier for investors to winnow the field of prospective fund choices. Because it typically takes a while for investors to adjust to new data, those who adopt trading costs estimates early and put them to use right away can gain a real advantage.

The data may also prove useful for fund companies themselves. Although many have an idea of their own funds' trading costs, they likely don't have a good measure of how they stack up against competitors'. I'm hoping this will lead fund companies to get smarter and look for ways to drive down their trading costs so that investors will enjoy better returns.

4

The Power of Expense Ratios Is Greater Than You Think

JACK BOGLE FRUSTRATES the heck out of people in the fund industry. The Vanguard founder is *always* talking about costs. He says you should buy low-cost funds, and other funds are a bad bet. He's always running new studies to prove his point. If someone comes up with a counterargument, he'll run a new test to disprove it.

Why does that bug folks in the investment world? Because those costs go straight to their wallets. The more a fund charges, the more it pays managers, brokers, mutual fund wholesalers, and big executives. Yet, the higher the cost, the worse the investment results, so there's an inverse relationship between expenses and performance. The fund company folks need to pay for that second home in Martha's Vineyard. They'd rather Bogle didn't point out this relationship. No wonder they're mad.

The other reason that Bogle's tenacity makes sense is that when logic battles greed, it needs to marshal all the resources it can to win. The longer I've been at Morningstar, the greater I appreciate Mr. Bogle's eloquent persistence. I've run scores of studies on costs in *Morningstar*® *FundInvestor*™, and yet readers regularly doubt whether costs really are that important. They'll call me or send me an e-mail saying, "I know costs are important but look at this high-cost fund that made a ton of money over the last three years; clearly costs don't matter if you get the right manager. . . ." Ugh!

Top 10 Worst Fund Ideas (I'm not making these up!)
1. Steadman Oceanographic
2. Kinetics Middle East Peace Fund
3. The Golf Fund
4. Morgan Stanley Dean Witter Best Ideas
5. Genomics.com Fund
6. Open Fund
7. Templeton Vietnam Opportunity
8. Westcott Nothing But Net Fund
9. Amerindo B2B
10. Marketocracy Masters 100

It's awfully tough to keep people focused on costs when someone else is flashing dollar signs in front of them. You see those big returns and imagine what you could do with all that money if only the fund could keep it up for another five years. In fact, the effect of imagining big bucks is very similar to the effects of a cocaine high, according to academic research profiled in Jason Zweig's book *Your Money and Your Brain*. No wonder people lose focus. Mountains of evidence to the contrary are no match for that buzz. It's like trying to sell fresh fruit on the same corner as a drug dealer. Not only that, but you don't have to write a check for your fund's expenses. The fund takes a little bit out of each day's net asset value so that you can barely notice.

I'm a contrarian who believes in the power of low costs. There's no particular strategy of investing that dominates my view. But underpinning everything is low costs. That doesn't mean indexing is the only answer. There are lots of low-cost actively managed funds and high-cost passive funds. In fact, Vanguard's actively managed funds have been just as successful as its index funds.

Let's take a look at how much expenses matter, and why.

Fund Expense Ratios Are So Powerful It's Sick

To twist a favorite saying of Woody Hayes, the Ohio State football legend, when you buy a high-cost fund, three things can happen, and two of those are bad. First, you can get good performance. Second, you can get underperformance. Third, the fund can perform poorly and then get merged away.

Yet, some people insist that costs aren't important because they remember only the first outcome. And, to be sure, there will always be some funds that manage to overcome high costs and outperform their peer group. There's Federated Kaufmann (KAUFX), for example, which has produced outstanding 15-year returns even though it charges 1.95 percent. The much more common examples are funds like Westcott Nothing But Net and Phoenix Nifty Fifty, both of which came out with high costs, produced poor performance, and then were put out of their misery. These funds' shareholders were among the very worst off: Their investment performed terribly and then they either got the remainder of their money back or their money was put in a fund they didn't want in the first place. In fact, liquidations and mergers often happen near the bottom, so that shareholders who don't act quickly to reinvest miss out on rallies.

Funds that don't survive are an important piece of the puzzle when you study the predictive power of expense ratios. With that in mind, I set out to look at survivorship rates of low-cost and high-cost funds so that I could get a true feel for your odds of success when picking funds of different expense ratios. Putting the pieces together that way led to a pretty stark picture.

Survivorship Bias, or Where High-Cost Funds Go

Many high-cost funds are simply mistakes that get swept under the rug. Costs, after all, reflect not just fee structure but asset size. A small fund with high costs is more likely to be unprofitable for the fund company (and therefore a better candidate for the scrap heap) than a large fund with low costs. In addition, higher-cost funds sometimes take on greater risk than they otherwise would in order to compensate for their cost disadvantage. In turn, they put up ugly numbers that can lead to them being merged away or liquidated.

Consider, for example, that all the technology funds in the cheapest quintile of their category in 1998 still existed five years later when the bear market in tech was ending and tech funds were rebounding sharply. However, 47 percent of tech funds in the priciest quintile were merged away or liquidated before the rebound.

The disparity is a little extreme, but the trend is borne out across the broad asset classes and within the individual categories. I looked at rolling 5- and 10-year periods from 1995 on to see whether high costs were a good predictor of whether a fund would be merged away or liquidated. Within each category, I separated funds into quintiles based on their costs, and I excluded categories in which there were fewer than five funds per quintile.

It turns out there's a high correlation between costs and survivorship, as high-cost funds had a striking attrition rate. For U.S.-stock funds, the cheapest group had an attrition rate of 13 percent over 5-year periods and 25 percent over 10-year periods. The attrition rate for the most expensive group was double that: Over 5-year periods, 29 percent of the high-cost funds had merged or liquidated, and nearly half (49 percent) had merged or liquidated over 10-year rolling periods.

The pattern was similar for international-stock funds and taxable-bond funds, though both groups had higher attrition rates across the board. For international-stock funds, the cheapest quintile had an attrition rate of 19 percent for 5-year periods and 33 percent for 10-year periods, while the attrition rates for the priciest quintile were 37 percent and 57 percent, respectively, for the 5- and 10-year periods. Taxable-bond funds in the cheapest quintile saw a 5-year attrition rate of 21 percent and 35 percent for 10 years, while the priciest quintile had a 5-year attrition rate of 37 percent and a 10-year attrition rate of 57 percent. The really striking part here is that not even half of those high-cost funds survived over a 10-year period.

All things being equal, funds with high costs are much more likely to produce poor performance because of their cost disadvantage. However, all things aren't equal, and most high-cost funds also have weaker management, higher-risk strategies, and fewer resources. Put that all together and you have a recipe for failure. When a fund comes out of the gate with a few years of bad performance, the fund company, realizing that it will have an awfully hard time attracting assets, kills it off.

How Costs Predict Success

Now that we've added the missing piece of attrition back in, we can see just how powerful expense ratios are as a predictor of performance. I again separated funds within each category into quintiles based on their costs, then checked on what percentage within each group managed to beat the category average. The category average overstates returns because it reflects only funds still in existence today. That's why even the best-performing quintile in our survivorship-free database saw slightly fewer than half its funds beat the official category average.

The results show just what a bad bet high-cost funds are. Funds in the cheapest quintile were more than twice as likely to succeed—that is, beat the average for their categories—than those in the most expensive quintile. Success declines rapidly as you move up in price. Of domestic-stock funds, 47 percent in the cheapest quintile succeeded over a 10-year period, 33 percent of the next-cheapest quintile succeeded, 30 percent of the middle quintile succeeded, 27 percent of the second-priciest quintile succeeded, and just 19 percent of the most expensive quintile beat the category average.

The pattern was similar in other asset classes. Among foreign-stock funds, those in the cheapest quintile were twice as likely to succeed as those in the priciest (40 percent to 18 percent). Cheapest-quintile bond funds were five or six times as likely to succeed (48 percent to 7 percent in taxable bonds and 49 percent to 9 percent in munis).

Your Chances Against a Cheap Index Fund

Those statistics are pretty compelling, but I also decided to look at how a fund's costs affect its chance of success versus a more formidable benchmark: the cheapest index fund in a category.

In particular, I looked at what percentage of funds within each cost quintile survived and beat the cheapest index fund in the category (see Table 4.1). It's a harder test to pass than the previous one, of course, because the cheapest index fund in a category is usually the cheapest fund of any kind, and index funds usually incur lower trading costs as well.

Table 4.1   Chances for Success When You Pick a Cheap Fund

Asset Class	vs. Priciest Quintile	vs. Second Priciest Quintile	vs. Mid- Quintile	vs. Second Cheapest Quintile
U.S. Stock	2.5x	1.7x	1.6x	1.4x
Intl Stock	2.2x	2.2x	1.7x	1.3x
Taxable Bond	6.9x	3.2x	2.3x	1.5x
Muni Bond	5.4x	3.1x	1.5x	1.1x

Data through end of April, 2008.

This table compares chances for success with cheapest-quintile funds versus other quintiles over 10-year period. It shows that you more than double your odds of success when you pick funds in the cheapest quintile over the priciest. Even going from the second cheapest quintile to the first boosts your odds by 10–50%.

Once more, we see that low-cost funds fared much better. The cheapest quintile of equity funds was nearly twice as likely to beat the cheap index fund as the highest-cost quintile. The cheapest quintile of bond funds was six times more likely to beat the index fund than the high-cost quintile.

The cheapest quintile of domestic-stock funds survived and beat the cheapest index fund 29 percent of the time, compared with just 17 percent for the most expensive quintile. For international-stock funds, we see a similar picture: 32 percent of foreign funds in the cheapest quintile survived and beat the cheapest index fund, while just 18 percent of the most expensive funds were successful. For taxable-bond funds, 19 percent of the cheapest quintile were successful over 10 years and a mere 3 percent of expensive bond funds succeeded. (There are no municipal-bond index funds to provide a benchmark test for tax-free funds.)

Low-Cost Funds Double Your Chances of Success

Factoring survivorship into the expense equation shows just how powerful expenses are as a predictor. Sure, there will always be exceptions. *Winning* lottery tickets are great investments—the catch is that you have no way of knowing if yours will be a winner. Fewer than 1 in a million win the jackpot. From a fund company's perspective, high-cost funds are like free lottery tickets, because the company has convinced investors to pay the bill. If the fund company is lucky, it'll produce returns big enough to attract large sums of money. If it isn't, it'll simply fold up the fund and hide its mistake under the rug. Of course, that doesn't make the losses of the fund's shareholders any less real.

Rather than making a bad gamble, the savvy investor should look for low-cost funds with sound fundamentals. Simply doing that will double or triple your chances of success and greatly reduce your chances of dramatic underperformance. In fact, Morningstar's Fund Analyst Picks apply those fundamental criteria, and they have succeeded about two thirds of the time.

As important as they are, expense ratios aren't the only thing. We'll discuss more quantitative and qualitative tests in later chapters.

FAQs

Q. Are 12b-1 fees included in expense ratios?

A. Yes.

Q. Which is more important: 12b-1 fees or expense ratios?

A. Expense ratios are what matters because they include any 12b-1 fees and are thus the real bottom line. How a fund's costs are divvied up isn't that important. Rather, it's the sum of the costs that matters.

Q. What's the difference between expense ratios in the annual report and those in the prospectus?

A. The annual report expense ratio tells you what the fund charged over the past fiscal year. The gross prospectus expense ratio tells you what the fund's total fees are currently, and the net prospectus expense ratio tells you what the fund's fees are after any subsidies. When you choose a fund, the prospectus net expense ratio is the best one to use, as it's the best prediction of future costs. You can find it on Morningstar.com and in *Morningstar FundInvestor*. However, the annual expense ratio is usually pretty close to the prospectus net expense ratio.

Q. Are mutual fund total returns reported before or after expenses?

A. After expenses.

Q. Why are bond fund expenses such strong predictors of performance?

A. Within a given bond fund category, the types of bonds that the funds invest in typically pay yields in rather tight ranges. Thus, returns before expenses are going to be in a fairly tight range. A fund with a 20-basis-point expense-ratio edge on most of its peers has a big advantage. It's just as important to save 20 basis points in a stock fund as a bond fund, but stocks' returns vary more widely, so it isn't quite as strong a predictor.

Conclusion

I called *costs* the skeleton key because they work everywhere. Bond funds, stock funds, gold funds—it doesn't matter. Start by limiting your search to funds with low expense ratios and low trading costs and you'll start way ahead of the game.

Think about it this way. If funds were like most goods, then paying up would get you better quality. But it doesn't work that way in the mutual fund world. Fund companies that have low costs tend to have good performance, and that good performance leads to lots of assets. Those assets, in turn, mean the fund company can reduce costs even further. In addition, these successful fund companies can lure many of the best managers because they have such large sums to run.

In addition, they have a much smaller hurdle rate to match or beat the returns of an index fund: Great managers might beat their benchmark by something like 100 or 150 basis points a year. But if you add in a 170 basis point expense ratio (or

(Continued)

1.70 percent of assets), none will do better than match an index fund with 20 basis points in expenses. So, what you need is a great fund that charges 80 basis points so that manager has a decent chance.

As the current decade has shown, you can't always count on big returns from the stock market. Sometimes returns are rather modest. The smaller they are, the bigger the bite that expense ratios will take in percentage terms.

I know it's hard to believe, but most of the time you actually get better managers at funds with lower expense ratios than you do at more expensive funds. Think about it this way. Would you rather be paid 1 percent of $20 billion or 2 percent of $200 million? The first scenario works out to $200 million and the second to just $4 million. Clearly, you'd rather have the $200 million than the $4 million if you want to maximize your profits. The mutual fund business is wonderfully scalable, so you're going to make way more money with the smaller slice of a big pie. Asset managers have to add some staff to keep pace with asset growth, but it doesn't require anywhere near equal sums. Therefore, lower-cost funds generally have better managers.

Some say that Albert Einstein said that compounding interest is the most powerful force in the world. There's some debate about whether or not he really said it, but I'd like to think it's true. When you pick low-cost funds, you are compounding more of the money you have saved. Given 20 years or more to percolate, that 50 or 100 basis points saved will add up to a handsome sum.

5

How to Use Total Returns Wisely

IT'S NO ACCIDENT that I waited until Chapter 5 to discuss performance, nor is it an accident that I'm instructing you on how to avoid a trap rather than suggesting that selecting past high-fliers is the way to riches. Yes, performance information is useful, but using a sort button to rank funds by returns is simply a bad idea.

I've established tests for manager investment, trading costs, and expense ratios, and now I'll walk you through a performance test. However, I want to be clear that the last test isn't as important as the first three. Nor will I suggest you sell everything that has had a weak three-year return and rush into the winners, even though that seems to be the answer that would satisfy many investors.

Using Returns Data Intelligently

Fund performance data are among the most useful data around—only not the way most people think.

Fund returns tell you a lot about how a fund behaves in different types of markets and it can help you to set realistic expectations. Is it as good an indicator of future returns as most people assume? Not so much. Unfortunately, it's the flash at the bazaar that draws investors' attention away from the important things.

Consider some funds that were outright performance champs at one time or another: Fidelity Select Home Finance (FSVLX), American Century Giftrust (TWGTX), Van Wagoner Emerging Growth (VWEGX), and Fidelity Magellan (FMAGX). They don't look so hot now, do they?

But you can use performance data for two things. For one, it can help you understand how a fund behaves in different markets, and secondly, you can use it to evaluate a manager's long-term record.

Look at a fund's trailing returns over the past 3-, 5-, 10-, and 15-year periods and you can see how it did versus its peer group and its index. That's helpful information. If it did well over the long-term periods, you may be on to something.

But don't stop there. Look at the calendar-year returns, too. There you'll see a richer, more complete story. Perhaps you'll see that even though the fund looks gangbusters right now it endured long stretches where it lagged its peers and index by huge margins.

You'll see times when it lost money. For a fund with a long track record, one of the easiest ways to get a handle on the downside is to look at its biggest losses. Obviously the fund could do even worse than its biggest loss, but at least you have some idea of what you'll need to be able to tolerate.

You can also check specific time periods to see how the fund did in different environments. There's the bear market of 2000 to 2002, the dotcom

Table 5.1   Annual Returns for Dodge & Cox

	1998	1999	2000	2001	2002	2003	2004	2005	2006	2007	08-08
Total Return %	5.4	20.2	16.3	9.3	-10.5	32.3	19.2	9.4	18.5	0.1	-14.5
+/− Index	-23.18	-0.83	25.4	21.2	11.6	3.7	8.3	4.5	2.7	-5.4	-3.11
% Rank in Category	88	6	15	3	4	18	4	18	47	62	75

Category Rank 1 = Best and 100 = Worst

mania of 1998 and 1999, the brutal banking downturns of 1990, and the credit crisis of 2007 to 2008. In bonds, you can look at 2002 when credit risk was punished and 2003 when credit rebounded so that credit risk was rewarded, or 1994 when interest rates surged. For foreign funds, there's the rise and fall of the dollar. It was strong in much of the 1990s through 2001 and again in 2005 but was weak from 2002 to 2004 and again from 2006 to 2007. A fund that hedges its currency exposure might have poor trailing returns, but if it performed well in 2005 and 2001 you know it might fare better when the dollar is strong.

Let's look at some examples. Table 5.1 shows Dodge & Cox Stock Fund's (DODFX) annual returns.

You can see that in 1998, the fund lagged the S&P 500 by a massive 23.6 percentage points and lagged nearly all its peers. In 1999, it was a hair behind the index and well ahead of most of its peers. But then look what happens after that. It runs off seven more top-quartile returns, making eight in total. That covers the bear market when it had just one losing year. That year was 2002, when it lost 10.5 percent, which was 1,160 basis points ahead of the index. Then, we see two off years in 2007 and the partial year of 2008. Should the slump have come as a surprise? Not really; we saw that it had a tough 1998, and if we went back further, we'd see more years like that in the past. That it would lose more in 2008 than any year of

Table 5.2   Annual Returns for Metropolitan West Total Return

	1998	1999	2000	2001	2002	2003	2004	2005	2006	2007	08-08
Total Return %	9.96	1.72	10.18	9.2	-1	13.9	5.2	3.1	7	6.3	-1.8
+/- Index	1.27	2.54	-1.45	0.7	-11.2	9.8	0.8	0.7	2.7	-0.7	-3.1
% Rank in Category	2	3	48	14	99	1	12	4	3	23	59

Category Rank 1= Best and 100=Worst

the bear market tells you that it's more vulnerable to a financials downturn than a momentum downturn. However, its 2008 losses were quite bad and understandably unnerving for investors. Although I understand why they'd sell, the past history tells you this might be a buying opportunity.

Now, let's take a look at a bond fund's past returns in Table 5.2.

MetWest Total Return (MWTRX) is an intermediate-term bond fund. The trailing returns for the 3-, 5-, and 10-year periods seem rather humdrum, as they range between 4 percent and 6 percent annualized as of August 2008. But look at the calendar-year rollercoaster. The fund lost 1 percent in 2002 and was in the bottom 2 percent of its category because it is more aggressive with lower-quality credits than most peers. But then it enjoyed a huge snapback in 2003 when the markets stabilized. It returned nearly 14 percent and was best in its category. Then as credit risk continued to be rewarded, it put up a string of top-quartile returns. Then, in 2008 when credit concerns returned, it lost money again and lagged, though much less dramatically than 2002. So, the picture being painted is a fairly aggressive fund that suffers losses when credit risk is punished but seems to get paid for it over the long term. This fund might be a good pick if you have a long-term time horizon, but it might not be the best choice if you have a time horizon of three years or less.

Now take a gander at Vanguard Growth Equity (VGEQX). It's a fund that was solely subadvised by momentum specialists Turner until 2008, when Vanguard gave part of the portfolio to another subadvisor (see Table 5.3).

Table 5.3   Annual Returns for Vanguard Growth Equity

	1998	1999	2000	2001	2002	2003	2004	2005	2006	2007	07-08
Total Return %	38.07	53.6	-23.1	-27.4	-30.9	38.6	5.4	7.9	6.1	22.5	-18
+/− Index	9.49	32.6	-14	-15.5	-8.8	9.9	-5.5	3	-9.7	17	-5.3
% Rank in Category	29	16	87	73	76	8	73	36	61	10	94

Category Rank 1 = Best and 100 = Worst

What's striking about these returns is that you can really set your watch by them. Turner seeks to have sector weightings equal to its growth benchmark but it owns faster-growing, higher-multiple stocks within those sectors. What that means is that when growth is on a roll, it slays the competition, but when growth is in trouble, Turner is in world of hurt. The 2000–2002 bear market was a perfect storm for that strategy, and you can see just how much downside this fund has by looking at those returns. Conversely, you can see the upside in growth-driven markets such as 1999, 2003, and 2007. It's also worth keeping past trends in perspective. The 1990s were kind to aggressive growth and the 2000s were awful. The next 10 years could be kind again. If you just looked at the past few years of returns, you'd figure this fund has no redeeming qualities, just as you'd have thought it was a great fund had you looked in 2000. Seeing the individual calendar-year ups and downs tells you the fund does at least make money consistently in good growth years.

Finally, the fact that there's now a second subadvisor whose approach differs from Turner's means that the past returns are a little less telling. Turner is still running part of the fund so there's some relevant information there, but it's no longer the whole story.

Using Performance to Pick Funds

Now that we've discussed how to use performance to understand funds' risks and rewards, let's look at how it works for predicting performance.

Top 10 Still Active Stock Pickers
1. Mason Hawkins and G. Staley Cates (Longleaf, LLPFX)
2. Schow, Kolokotrones, Fried (Vanguard Primecap Core, VPCCX)
3. Rob Goldfarb (Sequoia, SEQUX)
4. Ed Owens (Vanguard Health Care, VGHCX)
5. Joel Tillinghast (Fidelity Low-Priced Stock, FLPSX)
6. Charlie Dreifus (Royce Special, RYSEX)
7. David Williams (Columbia Value & Restructuring, UMBIX)
8. Will Danoff (Fidelity Contrafund, FCNTX)
9. Bruce Berkowitz (Fairholme, FAIRX)
10. Chris Davis and Ken Feinberg (Selected American, SLADX, and Davis NY Venture, NYVTX)

Unfortunately, short-term performance is of little use in picking a fund that you're going to hold for the long term. Simply put, there's too much noise there. Even the best managers have bad years, and the worst have good years.

To test how it works with funds that investors might consider, I looked at short-term performance of the 500 funds listed in *Morningstar FundInvestor*. As keeper of the list, I aim to select funds with good fundamentals, although I'll also allow some really big but bland funds just because people want to know about them. So, I wondered, how would short-term performance work within a subset of funds with pretty good fundamentals?

The answer is, funds with top trailing one- and three-year returns tend to continue doing well over the next short-term period, but fare poorly over the longer run. I grouped funds into quartiles based on past returns

Table 5.4   How the Success of Recent Winners Rapidly Fades Away

Asset Class	Winner Using 1-Year Returns		Winner Using Past 3-Year Returns	
	Next 3 Years	Next 5 Years	Next 3 Years	Next 5 Years
U.S. Stocks	1st Quartile	4th Quartile	1st Quartile	3rd Quartile
Foreign Stocks	1st Quartile	4th Quartile	2nd Quartile	4th Quartile
Balanced	1st Quartile	3rd Quartile	1st Quartile	1st Quartile
Taxable Bond	1st Quartile	3rd Quartile	2nd Quartile	4th Quartile
Municipal Bond	1st Quartile	2nd Quartile	2nd Quartile	1st Quartile

Data through end of April, 2008.

When you begin with a group of funds (The Morningstar 500) that has superior costs, management, and long-term records, the importance of recent returns is muted. Picking recent winners helps performance over three years but by five years that advantage has faded away. The good news is that in nearly every instance, each quartile outperformed most of its category peers because of their superior fundamentals.

within their categories and then looked out to future returns. It turns out that buying funds with one- or three-year returns in the top quartile generally led to strong performance for the next three years.

However, when you go out to the ensuing five years, the top quartile often did worst and the bottom quartile was just as likely to succeed. My chief conclusion is that short-term performance won't steer you to winning funds. It's also likely that there's a momentum effect in funds where hot sectors continue to be hot for a while—but then they correct, and the fund's returns peter out.

What about longer-term performance? Well, its predictive power works a little better, but even then, most studies have found only a slight link with future returns. In Table 5.4, you can see that if you picked funds from the first quartile of one- or three-year returns, you'd have felt pretty good for a while, but by five years out, the best quartile was usually overtaken. This is because markets rotate among favorites, and funds whose strategies once were in sync with the market later come back down to earth.

A better measure is returns starting from the day that the longest-tenured manager started on the fund all the way to present. I like the measure because it uses a long enough time period for skill to start to have an impact, but the period is limited to the manager's tenure so that you aren't stretching too far and using returns from previous managers.

I want a manager who has outperformed, but he doesn't have to have crushed his index—that could be a sign that his style has already had its day in the sun. Returns just ahead of the fund's benchmark will do.

Still, don't lose sight of the fact that trading costs and expense ratios are better predictors than past performance.

FAQs

Q. How long should I give an underperforming fund before I sell?

A. Wait until you're sure that the underperformance is a sign of deteriorating fundamentals. Consider the environment in which the fund underperformed and whether that underperformance makes sense given the biases of the strategy. In addition, look at performance since the manager took the helm. There would have to be serious problems to make me give greater weight to recent performance than performance since the manager's tenure started.

Q. What are the best benchmarks to judge fund performance?

A. Use a fund's index benchmark or its category average. If you're not sure what its benchmark index is, be careful to make sure you are using one that fits well with its investment universe. If a fund invests in small caps, you won't learn anything by comparing it with the S&P 500.

Q. What should I do if a fund has multiple comanagers?

A. It gets a little messy but the best option is to go back to the longest-tenured manager's start date. The longest-tenured one is often the lead manager.

Conclusion

Investors mistakenly treat returns like the standings in the sports section. See who's on top this year and you know who the best team is. But, it would be better to think of yourself as a scientist who wants to gather as much data as possible on a subject. How did the fund do in different environments, and what does the full body of evidence suggest?

Only very rarely do managers "lose it," as is often suggested after a bad year. They are just as smart as they were all along. When one of our favorite funds, Sequoia, reopened in early 2008, we said laudatory things about it but some readers insisted we were wrong, and that the real talent at Sequoia had departed, as evidenced by lackluster returns. But just a few months later, the fund had held up far better in the financial crisis than its peers, and it had top returns for 2008 and outstanding returns going back over the years. An investor stumbling across it might assume it had always looked brilliant. A few good or bad months can change three-year return rankings dramatically.

When you are itching to invest based on one year and throw out the past, invert your logic and ask, "Should I ignore past returns and focus just on this year? Do I want to overrule the weight of years of evidence for the most recent months, even though short-term performance is usually just noise?"

I'd answer no. You want to begin with funds that have low expense ratios, low trading costs, and high levels of manager investment. Then you should look for evidence of manager skill by examining the long-term record from the manager's start date. In addition, you can use past return records to set realistic expectations and understand when a fund should do well and when it will do poorly.

Be a scientist—not a sports reporter.

6

Understanding Mutual Fund Strategies and Fundamental Risk

To MAKE MUTUAL FUNDS work for you, you've got to understand their strategies and risks. Knowing a strategy enables you to properly evaluate performance, adopt reasonable expectations, and build a portfolio of funds that work together. We just discussed how looking at past returns can help you to set expectations. That's really the "what" side of the puzzle, and this is the "why."

This isn't part of the formula we'll use in picking funds, but it's a key piece of qualitative research that you need to know. I'll take you through the risks and the strategies so that you can invest wisely. You'll feel a lot more confident about your ability to invest when you can separate the deep-value strategies from the relative-value funds.

This and the following chapters will help you get a handle on the qualitative part of fund picking. When you buy a fund, you should understand what it does and be able to articulate why you bought it and why you'd sell it. One financial planner told me that when a new client brings him a portfolio, he doesn't know what he owns or why he owns it. The following chapters will help you to be sure you're not in that boat.

Fundamental Risks

All strategies have risks. After all, you don't get returns for taking on zero risk. The key is to understand them and be sure they are worth taking. Here are some key risks:

▶ *Concentration risk.* Funds with a high percentage of assets in their top holdings aren't necessarily riskier than other funds, but they can be. Some take on a lot of individual stock risk. For example, if a fund has a stock position over 10 percent or a few over 5 percent, it's more vulnerable to problems at an individual company than other funds would be. See Oakmark Select's (OAKLX) problems from a huge bet on Washington Mutual, for example. The fund had a 16 percent weighting in the stock when it was trading for around $50, and it didn't get out until around $3 or $4 a share, just before regulators seized Wamu. Interestingly, some other funds—such as Fairholme (FAIRX), Longleaf Partners (LLPFX), and FPA Capital (FPACX)—have muted that risk by holding a big cash stake.

▶ *Sector risk.* Besides having a lot in a single stock, a sizable weighting in a single sector runs big risks because sometimes everything in an industry goes in the tank at the same time. When a fund has more than 30 percent in a sector, it's courting sector risk. Marsico Focus (MFOCX) has significant stock risk, but manager Tom Marsico is careful to diversify among sectors so that one industry can't take the fund down.

Conversely, a slew of growth funds, including White Oak (WOGSX) had huge technology weightings in 1999 and were barbecued when the bear market hit. More recently, Clipper's (CFIMX) 50 percent weighting in financials hurt it in the financial meltdown of 2007–2008.

▶ *Price risk.* When a stock is trading for a high valuation, disappointing news will spur much larger losses than one with a low valuation. Essentially high valuation means high expectations. The 2000 to 2002 bear market was all about price risk. You had some sound companies whose stocks were trading at insane valuations of 75 or 100 times earnings, as though growth were limitless. When their growth slowed, the stocks got crushed, even though they were still growing faster than most companies. The further a fund is to the right side of the Morningstar Style Box, the greater the price risk.

▶ *Business risk.* At the heart of every stock fund is the risk that the businesses of the stocks they own will deteriorate. Some lose their competitive advantage; others see their whole industry collapse. Managers devote a lot of energy to avoiding these situations, but it happens to even the best of them.

▶ *Market risk.* Stocks and bonds lose money from time to time. That's how it works, so don't fire your manager for losing money in a bear market. Rather, you need to prepare your portfolio for occasional downturns by staying long-term and diversifying.

▶ *Credit risk.* Bond funds with corporate bonds or emerging-markets-government bonds are taking on some risk that the bonds will default. You can see this risk in the fund portfolio's overall credit rating. Investment grade runs from BBB to AAA and government. Below BBB are junk bonds. Funds with credit risk tend to enjoy smooth sailing for a few years, and then there will be a shock to the system and credit risk will be punished for a year or two before rebounding. In fact, the fear of defaults can lead to big losses for a fund even if it doesn't suffer defaults. For example, in 2002, the implosions of Enron and WorldCom led investors to avoid any corporate bond with any perceived weakness, and funds with large corporate bond stakes were hit hard. Most of these funds later rebounded to recoup their losses because the feared defaults didn't happen. Still, it illustrates the point that high-yield funds or any fund with a good chunk of junk bonds are suited for long-term holding periods even though we tend to think of bond funds as fit for shorter time periods.

▶ *Interest-rate risk.* This is the other side of bond fund risks. Interest-rate risk measures the extent to which a fund will get hit if interest rates rise. We measure this with duration. Typically, the lower the yield and the longer the maturity, the higher the interest-rate risk. Interest-rate and credit risk are sort of two sides to a teeter-totter. A junk bond fund has muted interest-rate risk because its yield compensates you for a pop in interest rates. A long-term Treasury fund has no credit risk but tons of interest-rate risk, as its low yield is little compensation when rates surge. Too many investors have made the mistake of thinking a fund with little or no credit risk has no risk at all.

▶ *Liquidity risk.* This is a more arcane concept, but when it does appear, it's ugly. The problem happens when a fund manager finds she can't sell her holdings easily and quickly. A fund with losses can slip into a terrible downward spiral if its holdings are so illiquid that its losses spur redemptions and then the redemptions spur more losses because the fund manager has to sell securities at fire-sale prices, and the cycle gains steam. In March 2008, you could see this happening at Schwab Yield-Plus (SWYPX), because its net asset value fell every single day, even when similar bond funds were up. The scary thing is that the fund's holdings were once quite liquid, but the market dried up.

▶ *Emerging-markets risk.* Emerging markets have outsized returns and outsized losses because they are based on rickety economies that work well in some environments but can fall apart in others. Every emerging market has been through brutal sell-offs. The risks are special because emerging markets tend to have less dependable rule of law where governments can seize company assets. Consider what the Russian and Venezuelan governments have done to oil companies that they don't like. Other times, we've seen emerging markets collapse because they were too dependent on outside financing, and once that money started to run away it had a domino effect.

▶ *Currency risk.* As I'm writing this, it doesn't feel like a risk from here in the heart of the United States. Currency risk means that if you have money in foreign currencies and they fall against the dollar, you lose money. Lately, the dollar has been pummeled and that has been a boon to foreign-stock and foreign-bond funds, most of which don't hedge their currency exposure. Still there are other times when the dollar has risen and taken a bite out of foreign-stock investors' returns. Before you invest in a foreign fund, find out if it hedges its currency exposure so you'll know what to expect.

Key Stock Fund Strategies

Now let's talk about strategies. When you read a description of a strategy or listen to a manager, pay particular attention to selling criteria. Depending on your personality and investing background, some strategies will sound clever and some will sound a little crazy. I have my own biases, but I've been watching long enough to know that most strategies have their merits and none are foolproof. Even the best strategies can be screwed up.

Likewise, every strategy is going to have ups and downs. The markets rotate favor among different strategies and sectors and no manager is immune to a down year or two. From Warren Buffett to Peter Lynch to Michael Price to the best team-managed funds at American and Dodge & Cox, you can find years when they were in the red or lagged the market by a wide margin. That's usually the best time to buy.

Regardless of the strategy, there are a few things to look for in every case. You want managers that stick to their guns and do not chase what's trendy at the moment. Yet you want them to remain diligent and keep an eye out for fundamental changes. The same goes for fund companies. Whenever value managers start getting fired and replaced with growth managers, you know value is about to have a great run, and vice versa. In short, you want discipline. If a fund is supposed to buy companies with accelerating earnings but it buys a distressed stock with declining earnings, it may be time to head for the exit. In addition, you want to see the manager excel at executing that strategy. If deep-value funds are having a great run but yours isn't keeping up with its peers, you should take a close look at whether there's a good reason for that.

For example, I was optimistic that Bob Stansky could do well at Fidelity Magellan (FMAGX) with his contrarian growth strategy. It wasn't on our recommended list, but I thought it was a pretty good fund. Essentially, the fund was so big that Stansky aimed to go against the flow on growth, so that he was buying when others wanted to sell. Thus, the fund's footprint would be fairly small. So, I was tolerant of weak returns from 2000 to 2002 because growth stocks were getting crushed and the fund was only a little off the pace of other growth funds. In addition, he had made a smart move into tech during a previous sell-off. But then in 2003, tech stocks were so cheap that they had a big rally, and Magellan was nowhere to be found. Stansky missed the boat, and that's when it was clear things were not working at Magellan.

Every manager will make mistakes, but if the manager makes a bunch of mistakes in an area that is supposed to be his expertise, that's a problem. If a fund's calling card is in-depth accounting analysis so that the managers know a company's balance sheet and business better than the rest, I'm going to worry if some major holdings have accounting scandals. Janus was supposed to be a fundamentals-driven growth shop, but it lost its shirt on Enron. Janus managers were buying near the top, which means not only did they miss the accounting tricks but also they looked at Enron's rapid growth rate and its huge P/E and said it could grow even faster to justify that huge valuation. They showed poor judgment in evaluating management, in understanding valuation, and in assessing risk.

It's also worth asking if the fund's past success can be repeated. When a strategy is working well, it often attracts lots of imitators who go after similar stocks and drive down the returns of the strategy. To get a fund with staying power, you need to find one that can do something better than others. Usually, that means something that is difficult or expensive to replicate. For example, Dodge & Cox, Wellington, and American Funds do better fundamental research than other big fund companies because they have a huge number of smart, experienced analysts who take ownership of their contributions to the firm. Everyone knows that and would like to be like them but it takes a ton of money and about 30 years to get there. Or in other cases, managers have developed a complex strategy that isn't easily imitated. That's what you want.

A Guide to Top Stock Fund Strategies

Let's take a look at some of the most important schools of thought on stock investing. I'll tell you some of the key adherents, the basics of the strategy, the usual sector biases, and the finer points of sell strategies. Some of these strategies are closely associated with a founding father, while others came from a few different investors, so I've labeled the latter with clear genealogy after the founding father.

Ben Graham's Deep-Value School

Ben Graham cut his teeth in the Depression when fundamental analysis was an unusual thing. So, he was focused on protecting against losses and found there was a lot of safety in buying very cheap stocks where you got something for almost nothing. A company with an asset such as land or cash worth $100 million whose market capitalization valued it at only $25 million was a good bet in Graham's eyes. Thus, buying a really undervalued, crummy company could be much safer than buying an apparently strong company whose shares could fall sharply just with a mildly disappointing earnings report. The catch today is that it's easy to run screens for some of those bargains so that they tend not to last. In addition, some of those deep-value stocks are cheap for a good reason, and therefore may not have the upside of better companies.

Typically, deep-value managers are buying industries when things look bleak and betting on a return to past norms. Thus, a deep-value stock doesn't have to transform into the greatest company in America to be a winner. At one of Morningstar's annual investment conferences, Jim Barrow said he hated many of the companies he owned. To make money, Barrow has to be able to figure out which companies are so poorly run (or inclined to cook the books) that management will run the company into the ground from those companies that have mediocre managers who won't miss the layups that come their way when the industry's fortunes turn for the better.

Nonetheless, this is a strategy that generally protects the downside pretty well, at the cost of some returns. Some of the best funds in this group have low-risk but marketlike returns. That sounds boring, but in down markets it can be beautiful, and over the long haul it can win. Many academic studies have found that value stocks outperform growth stocks over the long haul, although I wouldn't assume that it's guaranteed to be true over your particular investment horizon because what's in favor tends to rotate from year to year.

Selling

Most deep-value managers are patient, low-turnover investors, but when a stock rallies, they typically sell in order to keep price risk in check. Some, like Bob Rodriguez of FPA funds, are more willing to let their winners ride, and will hold stocks even as they move into the growth side of the Morningstar Style Box.

Risk

Business risk is a key risk. Managers' greatest fear is called a *value trap*. That refers to stocks that look like values based on their price relative to past earnings but the catch is that those earnings are going to continue to shrink rather than rebound. Low prices provide some margin for error, but if the business is a dud, it's still a bad investment. Think about airline stocks. One manager once quipped that it would be worth the money to pay someone full-time to remind him never to buy airline stocks. They often look cheap, but the industry's cutthroat pricing has made airline stocks a horrible investment.

Practitioners

These are Tweedy, Browne; Barrow Hanley (Vanguard Windsor II, VWNFX); Wellington's Philadelphia branch (Vanguard Windsor, VWNDX); Oakmark, except Bill Nygren; Charlie Dreifus (Royce Special, RYSEX); Bob Rodriguez of FPA, FPACX; John Rogers of Ariel, CAAPX; and Southeastern Asset Management (Longleaf, LLPFX).

Momentum Investing

This is the polar opposite of deep-value investing. Stocks that rise sharply have a tendency to continue rising for a while. In addition, companies whose earnings beat Wall Street quarterly earnings estimates tend to beat them the next quarter. These key observations are at the heart of momentum strategies.

The study of behavioral finance provides an explanation for why this works, even though it sounds kind of silly. Researchers have found that people consistently underestimate change in the investment world and elsewhere.

Say a company has a hot new product, and you expected profit margins to be 50 percent and earnings growth to be 15 percent. Instead, the company reports margins of 60 percent and profit growth of 20 percent, and the stock takes off. So, you might split the difference and boost your expectations to 55 percent and 18 percent for the next quarter, but instead you see 65 percent margins and 22 percent growth, and the momentum investors get a quick reward. Next, that hot product starts to cool off (see what happened to Motorola and the RAZR phone), and the trends worsen much faster than investors expected. The momentum investor gets out quickly, though not at the top because they waited until the first round of bad news came out.

Momentum managers are in a constant arms race. Lots of hedge funds, mutual funds, and day traders are testing out new wrinkles in momentum. Once something works, others pick up on it and the advantage is quickly squandered. In fact, some momentum models stop working as soon as they go from backtesting to the real world, so fickle is the world of momentum.

Watch how a fund sells stocks for a clue as to whether it's a momentum fund. Do stocks get tossed for even minor disappointments or fear of a minor disappointment? I once moderated a panel of growth managers and I asked them what they would do if they expected a holding to miss the next quarter's earnings estimates by one penny per share. The two growth-at-a-reasonable-price managers said they'd hold on, but Brandywine's Foster Friess said he'd dump it and look for something better. That's momentum in a nutshell.

Risk

Momentum can deliver big returns quickly, but man, is it risky. The reason is that these funds are loaded with price risk. When a momentum stock disappoints, it gets absolutely crushed. If you look at the track records of momentum funds, you'll see a wild mix of huge gains and big losses. So you either have to have great timing or a high pain threshold to make any money in them.

Practitioners

The Stowers of American Century were among the pioneers of this practice, and most of American Century's growth funds still have momentum components. Other prominent examples are Turner funds (Vanguard Growth Equity, VGEQX, Turner Mid Growth, TMGFX); Brandywine, BRWIX; and John Bogle Jr., BOGLX.

Valuation-Sensitive Growth

Looking for companies that are well run, growing at a healthy rate, and trading for less than the value of their businesses is hardly a novel concept. Scores of funds do some variation on this theme. Only a few do it really well. These sorts of stocks are the easiest ones for funds and brokers alike to sell their clients on, and they are researched heavily. The key is to find managers who dig deeper than the rest and have shown some skill at staying ahead of the curve despite the fact that the whole world is watching the same stocks.

The strategy is less risky than momentum, and in general, you get market-like downside. The only time I can recall these funds really getting hammered was from 2000 to 2002, when there were no growth stocks available at reasonable prices so that you had an unusual level of price risk in the stocks. Here are the characteristics of valuation-sensitive growth funds:

Risk

You get a little price risk and business risk here, but nothing extreme.

Selling

As you'd expect from this Goldilocksian strategy, some stocks should be sold because they are too hot and others because they are too cold. By that, I mean that some have rallied to where valuations are too pricey and others get tossed due to declining fundamentals.

Practitioners

Janus, T. Rowe Price, Fidelity, Putnam, American, MFS, Primecap, Ron Baron, Columbia Acorn, and Montag & Caldwell are among the many who have some funds that invest this way.

Black Box/Quantitative Strategies

Is it a good strategy to buy stocks with price momentum, low price/book, high levels of debt, CEOs near retirement age, and twice the volatility of the S&P 500? I have no idea, but you can be sure that someone has tested it, and if it worked in backtesting they are running it now. Companies have to report a tremendous amount of information to the investing public, and today there are legions of smart programmers armed with enormous computing power to crunch the data almost instantaneously. In fact, some funds are run using scores of models complete with another model to adjust the weightings of the other models based on how well they are performing. Quantitative strategies have to constantly evolve to keep ahead of the competition.

Quantitative managers don't like to reveal exactly what's in their models for fear that a competitor will use it. That makes such funds challenging for investors to use: You have to take a lot on faith. Some funds will at least tell you what part of the Style Box they aim to invest in, but they won't tell you their inputs, so when evaluating the fund, we have to place more emphasis on past performance than we're normally comfortable with.

When you're shopping for a quantitative fund, don't forget about the manager. Because the models need constant updating, quant-managed funds are just as likely as other funds to suffer declining performance when a manager leaves. Humans might not send in the trades at a quant fund, but they are responsible for adjusting the strategy. When longtime manager Chuck Albers left Guardian Park Avenue, the fund became mediocre rather quickly. Here are the characteristics of quant funds.

Risk

Quant strategies can go anywhere from value to growth, so the risks vary. However, there is one risk that really clobbers quantitative strategies across the board: Market shocks make beautiful quant models look really bad. The strategies are largely based on the idea that the past has some predictive value. They look at a company's past earnings and project trends, but sometimes the markets react faster than a model can. For example, quants had a tough go of it in 2007 and 2008 when oil prices exploded and financial giants melted down overnight. The spike was awful news for industries like airlines and autos and great news for oil companies and other energy companies. Traders quickly made back-of-the-envelope calculations on what each spike meant for those industries, but quantitative models were still going off past data. These data failed to reflect the current situation so that even flawed adjustments by humans were superior to programs using stale data. Making matters worse, the fact that hundreds of hedge funds use quant strategies meant that when leveraged hedge funds got squeezed, they were forced to sell en masse, and many quant mutual funds with similar holdings took it on the chin.

Practitioners

Some of the top quant managers are John Montgomery of Bridgeway, John Bogle Jr., Fidelity Disciplined Equity (FDEQX), and some American Century funds.

Warren Buffett: Great Companies at Fair Prices

Warren Buffett is probably the greatest investor in history, so it's kind of surprising that the number of managers trying to emulate Buffett is fairly small. Buffett began as a Ben Graham disciple, but his strategy evolved to tolerate paying a slightly higher price in exchange for a better company. In Buffett's words, he'd rather pay a fair price for a great company than a great price for a fair company. The reason is that a great company is a wise steward of its cash and can compound its earnings at a powerful rate over many years. That compounding will result in good long-term stock performance, provided you didn't pay too much to get the stock.

Buffett values a company based on the value of future cash flows and the barriers to entry, or *moats,* that keep competitors from doing the same thing. Two other key tenets are valuable whether you want to emulate the rest of his philosophy or not. First, you don't get many chances to buy great companies at fair prices and the damage from buying poor ones can be severe, so be patient and wait for the chance, no matter how long it takes. (He likes to say that unlike a baseball player, you can take as many pitches as you want until you find one you want to hit.) Second, he invests only in things he understands, so Dairy Queen, Coca-Cola, and GEICO qualify, and tech companies don't.

Selling

True Buffett followers sell only in extreme cases, such as when valuations get to sky-high levels or they simply acknowledge that they blew the call on fundamentals. Fund company executives and shareholders alike aren't always that patient. They want results now, and some managers find it hard to follow a strategy where success is measured in increments no smaller than a decade, while others are measuring quarters and years.

Risk

Buffett, and most who emulate him, courts a lot of concentration risk. Just one stock can really take a bite out of returns. Buffett argues that over the long haul, this concentration actually reduces risk because he's putting money into only the most attractive investments that should pay off over the long haul. That's true, but you have to be patient and also recognize that investing like Buffett isn't the same as investing as well as Buffett. There's only one Michael Jordan, and there's only one Warren Buffett.

Practitioners

Among the Buffett followers are Sequoia fund (SEQUX), which has long ties to Buffett, Chris Davis and Ken Feinberg of Davis/Selected and Clipper funds; Bruce Berkowitz of Fairholme Fund (FAIRX); Oak Value (OAKVX); Fayez Sarofim of Dreyfus Appreciation (DGAGX); and Mario Gabelli, Wally Weitz, and Bill Nygren of Oakmark (OAKMX). And of course, you can buy shares of Berkshire Hathaway and invest with the Oracle himself.

Peter Lynch: Buy Stocks That Go Up

The Fidelity school comes in many variations, but it really just comes down to buying stocks that go up. The firm has an army of analysts who uncover information that might not be reflected in stock prices. Some managers simply buy whatever stock has good prospects or has good news that is not priced in, regardless of whether it's a value or a growth stock. Essentially they want to invest anywhere they have information that the market does not. Maybe an analyst has found a pharmaceutical company with a promising drug that's misunderstood by the Street or maybe another portfolio manager sees signs that a bank's CEO is close to retirement and may be inclined to accept a merger proposal.

Risk

Like the strategy, the risks are all over the map depending on how each manager invests. Besides the usual stock fund risks like price risk and business risk, there's the risk that a manager will rotate out of a sector at the wrong time or the fund will end up with a lot of overlapping holdings with other investments in your portfolio.

Practitioners

Peter Lynch is one of the most influential managers at Fidelity, even though he has been retired for about 15 years. Today, managers like Will Danoff,

Joel Tillinghast, and Fergus Shiel have done a fine job of making this strategy work, although many more at Fidelity have produced mediocre results trying to do the same.

Vulture Investing

You could make a case for putting Marty Whitman and the rest of Third Avenue Value Funds in the Ben Graham camp, except that Whitman says Graham was wrong. So, Whitman and Third Avenue get their own little group. I'll include Michael Price disciples Mutual Series and David Winters, too, due to their vulture leanings. The strategy is to find super-cheap stocks—even distressed securities—that are so cheap that there is little downside. Most cheap and distressed stocks are in that state because they are awful, so it takes a lot of expertise and legwork to find the handful of good stocks that can be rehabilitated. The biggest difference with most Graham disciples is that Whitman buys companies that are near bankrupt or even buys the debt of those that are bankrupt. I like the approach because almost no one tries to do it. That's partly because it takes a lot of effort and partly because big fund companies don't want to have to explain to shareholders why they own shares of companies teetering on bankruptcy.

Risk

When a vulture investor is wrong, a holding often goes bankrupt. In addition, the strategy tends to have a fair amount of sector risk because adherents don't attempt to look like the market. On the plus side, price risk is minimal.

Selling

"We're not so sure how good we are at selling," Whitman once told me. As a result, he doesn't do much of it. He tends to hold until valuations get really high. He'll happily sit on a stock that could take years before its value is unlocked.

Practitioners

Third Avenue, Mutual Series, and David Winters (Wintergreen Fund, WGRNX) are included in this investing strategy.

Indexing

Indexing is all about costs. Index funds save money on two fronts. First, they don't have to pay for research, and second, they usually pay very little in trading costs because indexes are pretty stable. By paying less, you generally get better returns in the end. On average, an index fund will beat two thirds of its actively managed peers in a year but over time it can do a little better than that as the advantage compounds.

Indexing boasts a couple of other advantages. Index funds are very low-maintenance because you don't have to worry about manager changes or strategy changes. You can buy an index fund and forget it for a decade. Second, the low turnover of index funds means funds typically don't realize much in the way of capital gains, so they make good investments in taxable accounts.

When you are shopping for an index fund, look for three things: low expense ratios, low trading costs, and broad diversification. Many index funds don't offer all three, so be choosy just as you would with an actively managed fund.

Risk

Needless to say, you have lots of market risk and little concentration risk, unless you buy a sector index fund. So, the biggest risk is that the whole market is out of whack. For example, in 1999, the S&P 500 was a poor investment because tremendous speculation in large-cap tech stocks made the whole index rather pricey and tech-heavy. Fortunately, that doesn't happen too often.

Practitioners

The four best index players are Vanguard, Fidelity, Barclays (through its iShares ETFs), and DFA. Vanguard has the broadest lineup, and all funds boast low cost. Fidelity has four index funds that it is providing at expense ratios below costs. These four, which charge 0.10 percent, are the best deal going, provided you are investing between $10,000 and $100,000. They are Fidelity Spartan Total Market (FSTMX), Fidelity Spartan S&P 500 (FSMKX), Fidelity Spartan Extended Market (FSEMX), and Fidelity Spartan International Index (FSIIX). Above or below those investment levels, and Vanguard is the answer.

DFA is a special case. Its funds are passive, but technically are not index funds because they don't aim to precisely track an index. This flexibility enables DFA to lower trading costs to the point where it actually makes a profit on trades by being a provider of liquidity and putting the bid/ask spread to work for them. This is why DFA's small-cap indexes are the best around. The catch is that they are generally available only through planners who use index funds in virtually all of their portfolios. You can't just walk in to your Schwab or Smith Barney office and buy a DFA fund.

Top-Down and Bottom-Up

If you hear about a fund that's going to cleverly capitalize on major trends like the aging of America, run away. Most of these trend followers are terrible, in part because everyone knows about those trends. However, a few have actually succeeded at blending macroeconomic and industry analysis with individual stock selection. You can find that combination in a value or growth strategy, but it's more common in growth. Tom Marsico has done it brilliantly in his large-growth funds for 20 years. He adjusts sector weights based on his view about whether an industry has the wind at its back or in its face. That has led to timely shifts out of harm's way, but he backs it up with strong stock picking. Conversely, I've seen lots of thematic funds come out with lots of fanfare and then whimper off. AIM Dent Demographic's goal was to capitalize on big demographic trends, only it seemed more behind the curve than ahead of it.

Risk

You have market and sector risk. When a manager makes a good macro call you get startling results, and when the call is bad, the fund can be in last place. Even the great ones goof it up on occasion. Be sure to look for a long track record of successful execution and the ability to pick stocks well after the managers have identified the right trends.

Selling

Because there are a variety of ways to execute this strategy, the sell criteria won't be a dead giveaway. However, it will help you to see where on the value and growth spectrum the fund fits. That is to say, funds in this strategy usually also employ some selection discipline similar to one of the strategies explained previously. Beyond that, though, the funds' managers may also sell simply because they think a sector's run is over. For example, they might think that a slowing economy will hurt oil prices, leading them to sell all their energy stocks at the same time.

Practitioners

Some of the best at this game are Tom Marsico and others at Marsico funds, the international stock team at Julius Baer, and Oppenheimer's international group.

Top 10 Who Blend Top-Down with Bottom-Up
1. Tom Marsico, Marsico Focus (MFOCX)
2. Pell/Younes, Artio International Equity II (JETAX)
(Continued)

3. Ken Heebner, CGM Focus (CGMFX)

4. Dennis Stattman, Blackrock Global Allocation (MDLOX)

5. Oliver Kratz, DWS Global Thematic (SCOBX)

6. Bill Gross, PIMCO Total Return (PTTRX)

7. Dan Fuss, Loomis Sayles Bond (LSBRX)

8. Mark Yockey, Artisan International (ARTIX)

9. Bob Rodriguez, FPA Capital (FFPTX) and FPA New Income (FPNIX)

10. Steve Romick, FPA Crescent (FPACX)

Measuring Volatility

Now that we've looked at fundamental risks and strategies, let's review a more basic take on risk: volatility.

The handy thing about volatility is that you can measure it precisely and update it daily or monthly. Standard deviation tells you how much a fund moves either up or down. For example, an investor can compare two funds with the same average annual return of 10 percent, but with different standard deviations. The first fund has a standard deviation of 2.0, which means that 67 percent of the time its returns for the past 36 months have been between 8 percent and 12 percent. On the other hand, assume that the second fund has a standard deviation of 10.0 for the same period. This higher deviation indicates that 67 percent of the time this fund experienced returns between 0 percent and 20 percent. With the second fund, an investor might expect greater volatility.

Morningstar Risk is a similar measure, but it penalizes downside risk a bit more and is relative to a peer group. Specifically, it uses something called the *utility function,* which is based on the premise that investors would trade a little return potential for safety. It measures past performance over the trailing 3-, 5-, and 10-year periods.

Beta is a trickier one. It tells you about volatility relative to an index. By definition, the beta of the benchmark (in this case, an index) is 1.00. Accordingly, a fund with a 1.10 beta has performed 10 percent better than its benchmark index—after deducting the T-bill rate—than the index in up markets and 10 percent worse in down markets, assuming all other factors remain constant. Conversely, a beta of 0.85 indicates that the fund has performed 15 percent worse than the index in up markets and 15 percent better in down markets. The tricky part is that a low beta does not imply that the fund has a low level of volatility; rather, a low beta means only that the funds' market-related risk is low. In addition, betas change over time.

Putting Volatility Measures to Use

Because portfolio risk is the most important lens, I wouldn't rule out a fund just because its standard deviation is over a certain level. What's risky on an individual fund level might provide diversification that lowers risk for the portfolio as a whole. However, within a category where diversification values are similar, it makes sense to avoid those that earn a Morningstar Risk score of High—the top 10 percent—because you don't need to go to extremes, and investors have a hard time holding on to high-risk funds for the long haul.

FAQs

Q. Do fundamental managers employ quantitative screens?

A. Yes. Although I separated the pure quants, nearly every fund runs some screens and uses quantitative tools in other ways.

Q. How do you see what a fund is selling?

A. You can look at a fund's portfolio on www.morningstar.com and look for the stocks with the minus symbols next to their names. In addition, shareholder reports typically show stock sales and occasionally managers will explain why they sold a stock.

Q. Why do funds' turnover rates vary so widely?

A. Some managers use trading systems to move rapidly or will trade around a position as a stock moves up and down. Others say they are not good at selling and tend to hold on nearly forever.

Q. Should I own more than one fund with the same basic strategy?

A. You can, but be careful, because the funds may well move in unison. I'd suggest looking for funds that at least have some variations in the same strategy or possibly favor different sectors.

Q. How do I judge the risks of a new fund?

A. This is a time to lean heavily on the fundamental risk side. You may not have much to go on with volatility measures, but you can at least examine the portfolio and consider the risks. You could also look for a fund with a long track record and similar strategy to see what its downside was.

Conclusion

Diversification and a long-term time horizon mean it's okay to take on some risk. After all, you can't make money without doing so. You need to be smart about it, though. If you understand a fund's strategy and the portfolio, the fundamental risks should be clear. When you put funds together in a portfolio, consider how they will work together. Which will move in the same direction and which won't? Think about whether there are similar risks running through your portfolio. Do all your bond funds have lots of credit risk because you focused too much on yield? Do most of your stock funds have a bias toward one sector because that sector was hot when you chose your funds?

The value in thinking about fundamental risk is that it points out risks that might not be apparent in recent returns. A high-yield fund can go for years enjoying great returns, and then every once in a while it gets smacked as defaults surge. Knowing the risks will also help you to assess your funds when those risks do come home to roost.

As for volatility, avoid funds that have High Morningstar Risk or extreme risks. Make sure your time horizon matches the risk level. And remember that your investments are for the long term, so when one fund prints red ink you won't bail and miss the upside. For shorter-term needs such as expenditures in the next three years, use a money market account so that you won't have to worry about losing money in the short run. When you think about risks as well as returns, you're setting yourself up to navigate the right course through good markets and rough ones.

7

How to Find Good Managers and Avoid the Dodgy Ones

LET'S BE HONEST: Most investors decide who the best managers are by looking at returns and then building a rationale to justify picking the manager with the best returns. It's understandable; it's easier to measure returns than manager resumes or the shareholder letters they write.

But if you spend as much time as I do talking with managers and analysts, you know there's a better way. Instead of buying a fund, think of it this way: Hire great management teams with competitive advantages. No, you don't have to spend all day talking with managers. I'll share my insights from years of manager conversations.

Just because each fund gets one line in the newspaper and one data page on Morningstar.com, that doesn't mean they are equal. A manager working in the spare bedroom of his house might run one fund, and seven managers with the support of 60 analysts and 20 traders might run another. That's no exaggeration. A fellow analyst once called a fund manager and the phone was answered by his wife, who said he was out mowing the lawn. Yet, some people would happily plunk down a chunk of their retirement money to Lawnmower Guy if he put up good three-year returns.

I don't mean that a fund should have a minimum of five managers. One is fine. But you should think about the people behind the manager, including the analysts, the traders, and the fund company behind them. I know you have a life and you don't have managers' phone numbers so you can't fully do this on your own, but don't worry. I'll let you know what you can do to find good managers and I'll also share our research on the subject. In Chapters 10 and 11, I go in-depth to provide you the scoop on 30 fund companies.

What You Can Look For

We go out and visit fund companies and have the benefit of many visits to sort out who the smartest, most ethical management groups are. You can't do that, but you can read shareholder reports.

Look for managers who treat shareholders like partners. The best managers provide in-depth explanations for what they've done, and they own up to their mistakes. Some of the best in this respect are boutiques such as Longleaf, Third Avenue, Davis/Selected, and FPA. PIMCO, a fund giant, also posts fascinating articles to its Web site.

Another thing to look for is experience. You don't just want someone with gray hair. You want someone who learned from other great investors. It's not an accident that Warren Buffett attended the best investing classes in the country and learned from Ben Graham himself and had many brilliant classmates who went on to great careers themselves. Tell me a manager has Wellington or PIMCO on their resume, and I'm intrigued. Tell me a manager worked for Munder or Federated—not so much.

To confirm that you're on the right track, look at the fund company's other funds in the same asset class as the fund you are considering. This tells you about the support team around the manager. I know there's more than just one good manager at Fidelity's municipal-bond team, Wellington's domestic-stock team, PIMCO's taxable-bond team, and American's international stock team because their funds are strong across the board. Don't assume that strength in one asset class guarantees strength in another, however.

Top 10 Quant Funds
1. Bogle Small Growth (BOGLX)
2. Bridgeway Ultra-Small Company Market (BRSIX)
3. Oppenheimer Main Street (MSIGX)
4. Fidelity Disciplined Equity (FDEQX)
5. Bridgeway Small-Cap Growth (BRSGX)
6. Vanguard U.S. Value (VUVLX)
7. Janus Adviser INTECH Risk-Managed Growth (JDRAX)
8. American Century Income and Growth (BIGRX)
9. Vanguard Growth & Income (VQNPX)
10. Vanguard Asset Allocation (VAAPX)

Finding a Manager with Competitive Advantages

Whether you are looking for a stock or a mutual fund manager, you need one with competitive advantages. I've already spelled out some of these, such as expense ratios and trading costs, but you also want advantages in management. There should be some things they can do better than anyone else.

For example, some fund groups are experts in their niche. Calamos is one of the biggest and smartest convertible-bond investors. Security Capital is one of the biggest and best real estate investors. It has the experience, depth of analysts, and size that make it hard for others to match. Other fund companies can't afford to have as many analysts dedicated to those niches because they don't run as much money in the strategy.

Sometimes a competitive advantage is an involved strategy where you need experienced analysts steeped in its application. Third Avenue and Mutual Series have very particular ways of doing things, and their funds have consistently done well. They've built up teams of analysts who really know how to wade into controversial but cheap companies and find the handful of keepers. Those strategies are hard to replicate purely in a quantitative model. I believe most big fund companies are wary of such strategies because they involve controversy and occasional public arm-twisting. If you are a giant fund company trying for 401(k) accounts, you're not going to want any of your fund managers to be publicly pushing for the CEO of a potential client to be fired.

You don't become great overnight, and that gives great fund companies a huge advantage. American, Dodge & Cox, and Wellington are among the best fundamental investors because they have skilled experienced analysts and managers who are well paid, feel appreciated, and want to spend their careers at the firm. You can't quickly build a firm stocked with scores of investment professionals who have that level of experience and skill, nor could you quickly get them all working together. What's more, the brilliant, freshly minted MBAs are going to choose American and Wellington over a start-up because they know they will be learning from the best and have the potential to make a whole career there. Even if you were paying what they were paying you still couldn't match that offer. What all that means is that American, Dodge & Cox, Wellington, and a handful of other great shops have the human capital to be better fundamental investors than the rest of the world. That's a huge advantage.

Now turn that around and think about who doesn't have an edge. Many insurance companies and bank trust departments have competent investment professionals trained not to blow up clients. However, they aren't experts in any area. Their role in their company is pretty small, and the parent company is going to pay little attention to it, give it few resources, and not pay competitive salaries if that means upsetting a bunch of bankers or underwriters. The funds offered by banks and insurance companies are often dependent upon Wall Street research, so they are starting at a distinct disadvantage to firms with good analysts.

Take a look at all of your funds and ask what their competitive advantages are. No weak rationales such as, "This guy seems to have his finger on the pulse of the market." Or, "This fund invests in a hot sector that's going be huge. I can't recall the manager's name, but I'm sure he knows what he's doing."

Finding an Ethical Manager

You don't just want a skilled manager; you want one who will put your interests first.

Investing in funds with high ethical standards is the best protection from all sorts of actions that less scrupulous fund companies can pull that cost fundholders billions of dollars. Just as stocks with strong corporate governance outperform those with poor governance, funds with strong stewardship standards are likely to outperform over the long haul. We've created stewardship grades to make it easier to separate the good players from the bad.

There are lots of places where a fund company must choose between benefitting fundholders and boosting its short-term profits. For example, when a fund company sets fees, it's a pretty direct zero-sum game with shareholders. Deciding when to close a fund to new investors is another issue fraught with conflicts of interest. Closing a fund means a fund company is passing up fee income and therefore hurting its own short-term profits in order to avoid letting asset growth harm performance of the fund. Sometimes, fund companies act like Eagle Scouts and close the fund promptly, and other times they pretend the problem doesn't exist and allow the fund to get bloated. In the mid-1990s when Fidelity was the biggest fund company, it kept nearly all its biggest funds open.

That's why we created stewardship grades from A to F to make it easy for you to separate the good guys from the snake-oil vendors. You can find the grades on Morningstar.com, in *Morningstar FundInvestor*, and on this book's special Web site, www.morningstar.com/goto/fundspy.

We dig into filings to examine manager compensation, manager investments, director investments, fund board behavior, fund culture, regulatory run-ins, and more. We also visit companies and try to talk to a wide variety of people from sales executives, compliance officers, traders, analysts, managers, and directors. It's a very involved process, but we take all that information and boil it down to a letter grade so you know whom to trust. Just look for the A and B funds and avoid the Ds and Fs.

We place a big emphasis on corporate culture in the grade because it gets to the heart of the matter. Strong cultures usually have fund-performance-based manager-compensation plans, high levels of manager ownership of their funds, and reasonable expense ratios.

On the flip side, fund companies with weaker corporate cultures usually show poorly in other areas as well. Van Kampen's funds, for example, earned Ds (in 2008) for corporate culture for not consistently putting shareholders' interests before corporate interests. Also, many Van Kampen managers don't invest much in their funds.

We also rate fund boards based on the percentage of independent directors. I mentioned those conflicts of interest, such as fees and closing funds. Boards are key to resolving those conflicts in fundholders' favor. We look to see if the board has actively worked for fundholders rather than acted as a rubber stamp.

FAQs

Q. What should I do if a fund doesn't have a stewardship grade?

A. Start with an assumption that it's neutral—something like a C. If another fund you are considering is pretty similar but has an A or B, go with that. In addition, look for straightforward communication, low costs, and long manager tenure as signs that a fund company is a good steward.

Q. What's the curve of your stewardship grades?

A. We don't aim for a certain percentage in each grade, but the breakdown is A, 7 percent; B, 24 percent; C, 48 percent; D, 18 percent; and F, 3 percent. Because we devote most of our analytical resources to above-average funds, it's a fair bet that there would be much heavier weightings in Ds and Fs if we gave grades to all mutual funds.

Q. How do I know if a fund manager is hiding mistakes by selling stocks that lost a lot of money?

A. Check past shareholder reports and look at the portfolios. In doing so, you can also see if the manager praises a stock that later blew up.

Conclusion

When you choose a fund company, you're really deciding on who you want to trust with your retirement over the next 20, 30, or maybe 40 years. A lot will change over that time, but cultures tend to endure, and you don't want to mess around with your retirement.

(Continued)

Consider that many of the fund companies that lost the most in the bear market of 2000 to 2002 were also among those caught up in the market-timing scandal, including Putnam, Janus, Invesco, and AllianceBernstein. And most of the fund companies that did best for shareholders such as Dodge & Cox, Vanguard, American, and Longleaf didn't have any market timing or late trading.

The firms driven by short-term profits were also likely to take big risks in their portfolios in the hope that they could draw in more money. Why did Merrill Lynch and Strong launch Internet funds at the market top in March 2000? Why didn't American and Vanguard go for the quick buck and do the same? The good firms think about the long-term benefits of their shareholders. Their investment professionals saw that there was an Internet bubble and determined that investors were unlikely to use such funds wisely. On the flip side, other fund companies had marketing people in charge. They could think only about how big their bonuses would be if they brought in a few billion dollars in an Internet fund or allowed an aggressive-growth fund like Putnam OTC to buy extremely overvalued companies in the hope that the bubble wouldn't burst for another year.

In short, looking at culture and ethics through the stewardship grades leads you on the right path to the best fund companies.

8

The Inside Scoop on No-Load Fund Companies

FUND COMPANIES ARE as varied as fish in the sea. Some are huge, smooth-running corporate entities, others are one-man operations run out of a spare bedroom, and others are small boutiques of managers who want to manage money but not people. Some are a collection of disparate offices across the globe, and others have their founders' fingerprints on everything. (I always enjoyed visiting Strong Funds, where founder Dick Strong mandated that every screw in the building be turned so that the groove was vertical in order to avoid collecting dust, and some staircases were designated for going up and others for going down so that no one would bump into anyone while going the other way.)

Gaining a fuller understanding of each fund company is vital to the fund-selection process. You need to know in what ways the company is great and in what ways it stinks. Just because you're happy with a fund company's small-growth fund doesn't mean you should trust it to run a municipal-bond fund. Of all the fund companies out there, there's maybe one, at most, that has strong funds across the board. Lastly, it's important to know which fund companies have lots of manager turnover and which ones boast long-tenured managers you can depend on to be with you for the long haul.

Over my 15 years at Morningstar, I've visited scores of fund companies, and scores more have visited us in Chicago. In this chapter and the next, I'll share the insights I've gleaned over the years from these visits. In the previous chapters, I discussed quantitative measures that you can easily put to use in your selection of funds. However, this section covers qualitative insights that you'd find awfully tough to replicate unless you decided to quit your job and spend all your time visiting fund companies. We speak with virtually every fund manager out there, even though many won't speak with the press.

So, let's get right into it and look at how you can be a savvy consumer of each fund company. I've grouped fund companies into two groups—those that offer no-load funds and those that charge sales loads. If a fund company falls into both camps, I put it in the category under which the majority of its funds fall.

American Century

James Stowers II pioneered momentum investing about 50 years ago, when he started American Century.

The Kansas City–based shop has grown beyond momentum to run value and bond funds, too. It tends to run rather lean teams of three to five people dedicated to a couple of funds. Unfortunately, it has a mixed record of retaining top people, and there's a steady trickle of people leaving. As a result, American Century doesn't have a really strong competitive advantage.

Overall, the firm has a bunch of pretty good but not great funds. Most combine quantitative and qualitative work. The firm retains a soft spot for quirky black-box funds such as Newton and Veedot, which are the result of work in their quant labs. When American Century rolls these funds out to test them in the actual marketplace, the results often fall well short of their stellar performance in hypothetical situations. Don't fall for the "gee whiz" factor when there are more proven funds.

A new regime took over in 2007 and went to work on improving the firm's growth funds. There's certainly potential there, but I wouldn't rush in.

What to Buy: Phil Davidson's value funds and Glen Fogle's growth funds, such as Vista (TWCVX), have been solid performers. American Century also runs a decent low-cost gold fund, although gold ETFs have stolen its thunder. In addition, the firm runs some fine bond funds, but none that top my buy list.

What to Avoid: American Century Ultra (TWCUX) is under construction. American Century has changed its managers and strategy in the wake of dismal performance. Maybe it'll get things turned around, but it's rarely a good idea to rush into a fund where the "under construction" signs are up.

Artio

I know. It's just about the worst name in the world. *Artio* is Latin for bear, and the firm was spun off from Julius Baer. Get it? I can't help thinking this is the name of Coolio's sister. A new rule for naming fund companies: Don't put "bear" in your name, and don't go with a name that sounds like a pop diva.

But don't let the name throw you. This shop runs some great foreign-stock funds that blend top-down and bottom-up analysis. Artio International Equity I (JIEIX) (now closed) and Artio International Equity II (JETAX) (still open) have put up great results, thanks to managers Richard Pell and Rudolph-Riad Younes. The pair is a past winner of Morningstar's International-Stock Fund Manager of the Year award for consistently producing great results. When you consider all the ups and downs among sectors and countries, it's awfully hard to run a foreign-stock fund that consistently outperforms, but Pell and Younes have. The only difference between I and II is that II won't invest in small caps.

What to Buy: Artio International Equity II makes a good core holding.

Artisan

Artisan is a collection of great boutiques. Artisan has shown a knack for hiring good managers and giving them the tools they need to succeed. It has a bunch of autonomous little shops that do their thing and don't have to work together.

Artisan even has two groups of foreign-stock managers operating from different buildings in San Francisco. One is headed by Mark Yockey, who runs growth-style Artisan International (ARTIX) and Artisan International Small Cap (ARTSX). The other is run by Oakmark alumni David Samra and Dan O'Keefe, who run Artisan International Value (ARTKX) and the new Artisan Global Value (ARTGX) in a deep-value style.

I'm impressed by how strong Artisan's funds are across the board and the firm's ability to retain good talent.

What to Buy: It's tough to go wrong here, but Artisan International and Artisan International Value are two of the best. Artisan is good about closing funds before assets get too big, so sometimes you have to get in pretty quickly after a fund is launched.

Brandywine (a.k.a. Friess Associates)

This fund shop is strange, but its strategy is effective. The Brandywine version of momentum investing has proved to have staying power, while most other momentum funds have their moment and then become obsolete. The key is that Brandywine's momentum strategy is driven by humans, not computers.

Nearly every other momentum strategy lets computers do all or nearly all of the lifting. The advantage of that method is that computers can process enormous volumes of data very quickly, so they can test new strategies and make actual trades faster than a human can. The catch is that there are scores of smart programmers at hedge funds, mutual funds, pension funds, and elsewhere, all trying to do the same thing. The power of a clever new strategy rapidly fades as others spot the same thing and the advantage is nullified. In fact, some momentum quants have lately tried to move in a more fundamental direction because of those diminishing returns.

Brandywine's edge is that it instead employs a big crew of analysts to canvas the world for human intelligence. That's much harder to replicate. The analysts do a lot of "channel checks" to figure out how a company's sales are working out before Wall Street does. They'll talk with car dealers, retailers, doctors, and the like to get the latest dish. If they hear signs of weakness, they'll dump the stock in heartbeat and move on to something better. As a result, they've done a nice job staying ahead of the game as the fortunes of one sector wane while those of another are on the rise.

The culture is unusual. It feels very much like a wholesome tight-knit family, yet the employees aim to limit communication to the bare essentials by using e-mail and writing as short a message as humanly possible.

What to Buy: Brandywine has two flavors, mid-growth/large growth (Brandywine, BRWIX) and large growth (Brandywine Blue, BLUEX), and they're both good. The funds run very high turnover, which leads to capital gains payouts, however, so they're good for only IRAs and 401(k)s.

Bridgeway

Bridgeway is a new-age fund company. It gives a big chunk of its profits to charity, keeps costs low, and makes many decisions as a group. That may be a little touchy-feely, but it beats investing with a shop run by cynical money-grubbing sharks.

I love the firm's commitment to its shareholders and low costs. John Montgomery is an engineer who builds clever quantitative models for picking stocks in a variety of strategies. Bridgeway also runs some index funds.

What to Buy: Montgomery ran a study that found the best strategy is to buy the funds with the worst recent performance, although shareholders were of course doing the opposite. So, look for one in a slump and buy it.

Dodge & Cox

I love the business model here. Dodge & Cox is owned exclusively by employees. When they retire, they have to sell back their shares at a set multiple. That's a great setup that ensures independence and a long-term focus, as well as good succession planning.

One of the best investment groups around, Dodge essentially has three portfolios: domestic stock, foreign stock, and bonds. It also offers a global-stock fund and a balanced fund that are essentially combinations of two of the three core portfolios.

Dodge does a great job of attracting and retaining top talent. Most spend their whole career at Dodge. Dodge is very patient with analysts and gives them time to learn the job properly. In fact, the company doesn't even monitor the success of the analysts' picks at first. The firm runs its funds with a *team* of managers, so investors have tremendous stability year in and year out.

The core strategy is to look for well-run companies at good value prices. The managers will sometimes switch within an industry from a company where everything is going right and its high multiple reflects that, to one with low expectations and greater potential.

Dodge is willing to close its funds if asset growth becomes a problem, but currently all the funds are open because a brutal slump in 2008 has led to redemptions. But don't worry; an off-year is to be expected, and I see no reason to bail.

What to Buy: Any of them. I own International (DODFX) but if I were starting over I'd probably buy the recently launched Global Stock (DODWX) because of the greater reach it affords management.

Fidelity

This is still very much Ned Johnson's shop. He wants to be the biggest and best. Those under him who don't deliver that are shown the door. Fidelity invented the star manager, and the house that Peter Lynch built still treats managers like gods. Most funds have just one manager, but they tend not to stay for long. Funds under $10 billion tend to lose their managers to the bigger funds, so funds are frequently in transition. Making matters worse is that few managers stick around past their forty-fifth birthday, no doubt in part because so much depends on them. In short, this is no company for old men.

Maybe the oddest thing about the Boston Behemoth is that it really doesn't have an investing philosophy. If there is one, it would be summarized by Oakland Raiders owner Al Davis's, "Just Win, Baby." In other words, just pick stocks that go up, because if you stick to an investment discipline and that discipline is out of favor for three years, you might be toast. So while managers tend to fall into value, blend, and growth camps, you won't see a distinct ingrained strategy such as Longleaf's deep value, American Century's momentum, or anything else. So oddly, the house of Lynch just isn't that good at running equity funds. If you do buy an actively managed stock fund, keep it in a tax-sheltered account so that you can follow the manager as he/she passes through to different funds.

On the plus side, Fidelity has a culture that lets quirky investors thrive. Managers don't have to go out to market their funds to brokers, so they can spend all their time running their funds. Thus, they have some nerdy quiet types who love to pick stocks and are quite happy there.

The key development to watch is Fidelity's effort to upgrade its analyst staff—something as ambitious and far-reaching as Boston's Big Dig. Fido fell way behind the competition when it comes to building an analyst staff. The old way was to rotate analysts through a wide range of two-year sector assignments so that they could one day become portfolio managers. Needless to say, having an insurance analyst with 10 months' experience competing with insurance analysts with 10 or 20 years' experience from other top fund companies puts Fidelity at a big disadvantage. Those firms put analysts on a par with managers and let them choose whether they want to be managers or analysts.

Fidelity was able to get away with that system when it was legal for companies to provide earnings guidance to their biggest investors before they shared it with the investing public. Then Regulation Fair Disclosure (Reg FD) banned the practice, and Fidelity's poor research efforts were exposed.

So, in 2006 Fidelity decided to try to have senior analysts of its own and it hired a slew of experienced analysts for the first time. That big bang caused a lot of upset at the firm, but it may yet pay off down the road. I won't be a big fan of Fidelity's stock funds until I see signs that this effort is really paying off. In fact, 2008 has proved to be a very tough year for a lot of Fidelity's stock funds, so I'm still waiting for signs of spring.

What to Buy: Fidelity's muni funds are the real gems here. (Sorry, Mr. Lynch.) They do a great job of doing high-quality research without taking big bets. For my money, Fidelity and Vanguard are the only answers in munis. On the taxable-bond front, Fidelity has some good high-yield funds. It also has decent high-quality taxable-bond funds, but some got burned by subprime mortgages in 2007.

On the equity side, there are some good options, but don't go whole hog. Fidelity has four index funds that charge just 0.10 percent, making them the best bargains in indexing. Fidelity also has some great managers, but many of them run funds with asset bases so big that it takes a little of the appeal away. Remember, these are solo managers, so there are very real limits to what they can run effectively. The best of these are Will Danoff's Contrafund (FCNTX) and Larry Raker's Dividend Growth Fund (FDGFX). I also like John Dowd's energy funds. He's an experienced energy analyst that Fidelity hired away from Bernstein. He runs Fidelity Select Energy Service (FSENX) and Fidelity Select Energy (FSESX).

What to Avoid: Most of the equity funds are mediocre. Some of the Select funds now have seasoned analysts who actually plan to stay at their funds. If you aren't sure about whether a Select fund is run by one of those, stay away. One way to tell is to look at the funds they managed in the past. If the manager of a tech fund was formerly running a transportation fund, take a pass.

Harbor Funds

Harbor farms out all of its management duties to other firms and it charges a reasonable fee for it. Its cheaper share class is labeled institutional, but the minimum investment is only $1,000 for bond funds and $50,000 for stock funds, so don't be put off by the name.

Harbor has hired some great managers, including Hakan Castegren, Bill Gross, and Sig Segalas. However, there are also some clunkers, so don't plunge into a Harbor-branded fund you don't know just because you liked a different one.

What to Buy: On the bond side, look for PIMCO-run funds Harbor Bond (HABDX) and Harbor Real Return Bond (HARRX). On the stock side, International (HAINX), International Growth (HIIGX), and Capital Appreciation are all standouts. There's also a great commodity fund, Harbor Commodity Real Return Strategy (HACMX), which is run by PIMCO and was launched in September 2008.

What to Avoid: Harbor SMID Value (HISMX) is off to a rough start (perhaps because "SMID" isn't a word) so I'd wait for the ship to be steadied.

Harbor sometimes takes a chance on less-proven managers like the SMID fund's managers.

Janus

Oh boy! I could fill two books with Janus stories. There's lots of drama and a rise and fall that make Mount Everest look puny. I can't get into it all in this space, but I will share my favorite PR quote ever. In a magazine article that recounted stories about founder Tom Bailey's wilder days in which he and friends had an annual drug-infested weekend nicknamed the Bob Dope Classic, a PR person said: "What does Tom Bailey's sleazy past have to do with anything?" Give her a raise!

Today, nearly all of the first and even second wave of managers to build Janus have gone and the firm has ridden a tremendous boom, bust, and boom phase to get where it is today. So, put aside your idea of the old Janus and take a look with fresh eyes.

In the wake of a scandal and terrible performance in the bear market of 2000 to 2002, Gary Black came in from Goldman Sachs and made Janus strong once more. He built up a good analyst staff that covered way more stocks than before. In elevating analysts and bringing sanity to the way bonuses were paid, he unfortunately drove away some good managers. However, you wouldn't know it from performance. Janus had outstanding performance in recent years. If it can do a better job of retaining managers, it could sustain its strong recent performance.

What to Buy: Look for one of Janus's experienced managers, such as Ron Sachs, who took over Janus Twenty (JAVLX) in 2008, or David Decker, who runs Contrarian (JSVAX). In addition, Janus has two strong partially owned subsidiaries in quantitative risk-managed experts INTECH and fundamental value shop Perkins, Wolf, McDonnell & Co. Perkins's Janus Mid Value (JMCVX) is a great straightforward value fund.

What to Avoid: There are no real dogs at Janus, but some of its advisor-sold shares are kind of pricey and some of its funds have inexperienced managers.

Longleaf Partners (a.k.a. Southeastern Asset Management)

Memphis-based Longleaf embodies long-term investing. Managers Mason Hawkins, Staley Cates, Jason Dunn, and Andrew McDermott invest nearly all their money in their funds, and they manage with a singular focus on producing strong long-term results. They run a focused value strategy that hits bumps along the way but they consider that the cost of ensuring acceptable long-term returns. Their long-term record is outstanding.

One of my favorite things about the managers at Longleaf is the way they communicate with shareholders. They actually treat them like partners and explain the failures, successes, and their thinking about the current portfolio. If you want to see what good shareholder reports look like, go to: www.longleafpartners.com/funds/partners_reports.cfm.

What to Buy: Longleaf only runs three funds and one is closed, so consider the other two—Longleaf Partners (LLPFX) and Longleaf Partners International (LLINX).

Loomis Sayles

Loomis Sayles Bond fund (LSBRX) manager Dan Fuss is kind of like the Warren Buffett of bonds. He is unassuming, insightful, and he's got a remarkable, very long track record. His fund is a bold, wide-ranging fund that can invest anywhere on the globe. Unlike others with that mandate, he hasn't forgotten about protecting investors' principal, so that the fund's losses are usually brief and mild.

Loomis also has some other good bond funds and some decent stock funds. The other bond funds are bold but not as wide-ranging as Loomis Sayles Bond.

What to Buy: Besides Loomis Sayles Bond, the firm offers a good dedicated international-bond fund in Loomis Sayles Global Bond (LSGLX). With either one, you should have a minimum time horizon of at least five years. Don't expect stable money market–like performance and you should be fine.

Marsico

Marsico does an excellent job of blending top-down macroeconomic analysis with bottom-up growth stock selection. Firm founder Tom Marsico has brought along other promising managers to apply that same strategy to foreign stocks and mid-cap U.S. stocks, so that the firm now boasts a stable of appealing funds, albeit running pretty much the same strategy.

Marsico Focus (MFOCX) is the firm's flagship, and as he did with his former charge, Janus Twenty, Tom Marsico has shown a knack for running a concentrated growth portfolio with great potential while staying mindful of the risks. Although aggressive, Marsico limits his sector bets and price risk (the risk of holding a company with high valuations when it disappoints the market) because having a focused portfolio of growth stocks is plenty risky as it is.

My one gripe is that, despite huge asset bases, most of the funds still have relatively high costs.

What to Buy: The best way to Marsico is through the back door. You can actually get lower costs by buying a fund run by Marsico but operated by someone else. Harbor International Growth (HIIGX) is a lower-cost version of James Gendelman's Marsico International Growth. USAA Aggressive Growth (USAUX) is a lower-cost version of Marsico Growth, and you don't have to be a member of USAA to buy it.

Masters' Funds

Litman/Gregory offers a clever alternative route to diversification. It hires three to five subadvisors from outside firms who pick their best 10 stocks to make up the portfolio. That way, you get diversification into different strategies without ending up with 1,000 stocks across five funds. Litman/ Gregory has done a great job of picking good managers and being patient with them when appropriate, but also firing those who aren't working out. It has also shown it will close a fund before it gets too big.

What to Buy: Equity (MSEFX), International (MSILX), and Smaller Companies (MSSFX) all offer outstanding managers and a reasonable price.

Matthews Asia Funds

When you buy a regional fund or a sector fund, you want expertise in the field, and that's what you get here but rarely elsewhere. Matthews invests only in Asia, and it has built strong records and a sizable staff of Asia experts. In addition, its funds tend to be fairly reasonably priced, while most Asia specialty funds have horrendously high expense ratios.

What to Buy: Asia's emerging markets pack plenty of risk, so don't go overboard. Choose a broad regional fund rather than one of the firm's single-country funds. Limit yourself to one fund and keep that fund to 5 percent of your portfolio or less. Beyond that, look for lower expenses and a fund with a risk profile you can tolerate. Look at its calendar-year returns and see if you would hold on through the worst calendar-year loss.

Oakmark (a.k.a. Harris Associates)

Oakmark does value, and that's about it. Oakmark wisely avoided expanding into bonds or growth stocks. Most of the funds are run in a deep-value, fairly focused style, with the exception of Bill Nygren's funds, which are more relative value. *Deep value* means buying stocks at very low valuations with the idea that either the company will right itself or the industry it is in will rebound. It takes patience, but it is effective. Nygren, by contrast, is willing to pay a little more for companies he considers excellent.

Oakmark's funds have strong long-term records across the board. However, Nygren had a rough 2005 and 2007 at Oakmark Select and Oakmark

Fund, and man, do we get angry e-mails whenever we say anything nice
about him! Nygren didn't see the bursting of the housing bubble coming,
and it hit him like a freight train—especially in Select, where Washington
Mutual soaked up more than 16 percent of assets at its peak. That's disappointing, but his long-term record is still strong and he's a good fundamental investor, so I still own the fund and recommend it. We stuck by
Oakmark fund in 1999 and 2000 when everyone hated it then, too, and it
came back strongly. I'm hoping we're in for a repeat, but I understand why
folks have lost patience. But in fact, in 2008 through October, it held up
much better than the S&P 500 when the market tanked.

Oakmark has shown it can manage foreign-value portfolios as
well as domestic value as its foreign and global funds have been its best
performers.

What to Buy: David Herro's Oakmark International (OAKIX), Nygren's
Oakmark Fund (OAKMX), Oakmark Global (OAKGX) run by Clyde
McGregor and Rob Taylor, and Oakmark Equity & Income (OAKBX) run
by McGregor and Ed Studzinski are all good bets.

PIMCO

Most of the best taxable-bond shops are primarily institutional ones like
PIMCO. That's because institutions such as pension funds demanded
more discipline and sophistication than mutual funds did. Now everyone
wants to be like PIMCO, but few are in its league. That's why it runs the
biggest bond fund in the world: PIMCO Total Return (PTTRX). It also
owns such a large slice of emerging-markets bonds that it's a rock star in
Latin America.

PIMCO's approach is to stay ahead of the curve on big macroeconomic
issues and to outwork the competition by having more and better analysts and sector specialists. PIMCO adds value through issue selection, but
because it is so big, the main things it does are large-scale bets that can be

done with billions of dollars. That means things such as predicting the direction of interest rates, selecting the spot on the yield curve that's most attractive, and choosing the best sectors such as mortgages versus Treasuries versus corporate bonds. Making those choices accurately is incredibly hard to do, but PIMCO is very good at it.

If you buy a PIMCO fund, be prepared for a rather unusual-looking portfolio. PIMCO is a big fan of futures, in part because they are easy to trade in bulk. So, you end up with some strange composition figures that might show a lot in cash or other, but the actual underlying holdings aren't all that exotic. Although subprime mortgages and other crazy derivatives have blown up at other fund companies, PIMCO has shown so far that it knows what it's doing here.

PIMCO boasts quite a few bond luminaries, such as Bill Gross, Mohamed El-Erian (who ran Harvard's endowment fund for a year before returning to PIMCO), and Paul McCulley. Even former Fed chairman Alan Greenspan is on the payroll as a consultant.

Now that I've told you how awesome PIMCO is, I have some bad news. It gives institutions a fair deal on expense ratios but its load and no-load funds for the masses are much pricier. Fortunately, there are two good ways to make an end run around that problem. First, PIMCO Total Return's strategy is available in two low-minimum funds with smaller expense ratios: Harbor Bond (HABDX) and Managers Fremont Bond (MBDFX). Second, you can buy many of PIMCO's institutional share classes through fund supermarkets such as Schwab and Fidelity for a set fee. To find out if the fee is worth paying, just divide the fee by the amount you are investing and the years you expect to hold the fund. Then add that sum to the institutional expense ratio and compare it with the D shares. If you are investing more than $100,000, then the institutional share class is probably the way to go.

What to Buy: For a core holding, Harbor Bond or Managers Fremont Bond are great. Harbor Real Return offers PIMCO's TIPS strategy.

In addition, PIMCO Foreign Bond (available with a currency hedge and without) and PIMCO Emerging Market Bond (PEMDX) are great options if you can get into the institutional share class.

What to Avoid: Don't buy the A or D shares of PIMCO Total Return because you can save money with either the Harbor or Managers fund.

Primecap

Probably my favorite growth manager, Primecap was formed in 1983 when its managers left American Funds to set out on their own. Primecap's management style is reminiscent of American. You have a big team of experienced analysts and managers who apply a sound approach of doing in-depth analysis of growth stocks. As at American, most make a career out of it because of the healthy culture and the fact that investment professionals own the firm. Primecap subadvises three Vanguard funds and runs three with its own Primecap Odyssey label that you can buy from Primecap directly.

Too many growth managers are focused on the next quarter or do flimsy buzzword-based investing, but Primecap's patient, contrarian approach to growth has led to outstanding results. Consider 1999 and 2000: Vanguard Capital Opportunity (VHCOX) earned a 98 percent return on the strength of tech and health-care stocks. In 2000, most funds that earned a huge return in 1999 were crushed when the Internet bubble burst, but Primecap's focus on fundamentals and valuations enabled it to gain 18 percent that year. Once again in 2008 Primecap's funds held up far better than the rest of the growth fund world.

What to Buy: Two of Primecap's three Vanguard funds are closed. The third, Vanguard Primecap Core (VPCCX), is an outstanding low-cost large-growth fund. Among Odyssey funds, Primecap Odyssey Aggressive Growth (POAGX) is the best choice because its small/mid-cap focus means it has little overlap with Primecap Core.

Royce

The Hitchhikers' Guide to the Galaxy describes a guy who is a rain god (but he doesn't know it) and has 17 different names for the different types of rain. Substitute small-value for rain and you've got Royce in a nutshell. It has a slew of funds that all invest in small-value or something close. Sure, some of the funds are in the small-blend slot of the Style Box and others are micro-cap value or small and mid-cap value, but they don't stray too far from home.

What to Buy: The key to understanding Royce is that each manager is largely on his own, so you want to keep an eye on how much money the manager runs in total. Although the managers' low-turnover style helps, you still don't want a huge fund because small-value stocks don't have a lot of trading volume. My favorite is Royce Special Equity (RYSEX), which is run by Charlie Dreifus. It's his only fund, and he has shown he's willing to close it in a timely way. Dreifus is an accounting stickler, and he'll buy only companies with clean balance sheets. The fund tends to lag in rallies and make up ground in downturns.

T. Rowe Price

T. Rowe Price's core philosophy is to produce attractive returns with moderate risk. T. Rowe recognized long before most people that fund investors do better in funds with moderate risks because they'll stick with the funds rather than hopping in and out. You can spot a T. Rowe portfolio from a mile away. It is well-diversified by sector and stock so that it provides a smooth ride. T. Rowe also provides stability in management and strategy. Its funds do what they say they're going to do, and that doesn't change when the managers change. In addition, the funds don't have many manager changes, and when they do, they are well-orchestrated, gradual transitions. (You hear that, Fidelity?)

T. Rowe has a fund of just about every flavor you can imagine, and nearly all of them are pretty good. T. Rowe has modest expense ratios and is a good, trustworthy steward of other people's money. It will close funds when they get big, but they don't close super early like Wasatch.

What to Buy: It's hard to go wrong with a T. Rowe fund. U.S. stock funds are the firm's strongest suit, so take a look at Brian Rogers' Equity Income (PRFDX), Dividend Growth (PRDGX), New America Growth (PRWAX), and Capital Appreciation (PRWCX). The firm has been working to improve its rather mediocre broadly diversified foreign funds, and now Global Stock (PRGSX), run by Rob Gensler, is a standout. It's not too big, and Gensler, who has built a great record at other funds he ran before this one, is making full use of his flexibility to go anywhere. On the bond front, High-Yield (PRHYX) and Spectrum Income (RPSIX) are among the best.

What to Avoid: T. Rowe's index funds seem like an afterthought and it charges more than Vanguard and Fidelity.

Third Avenue (a.k.a. M.J. Whitman Co.)

Third Avenue runs a distinctive value strategy that courses throughout its funds. The firm's mantra is "safe and cheap." Whitman believes many of the safest stocks are those whose outlooks look so awful that the stock is dirt-cheap and has nowhere to go but up. As Whitman says, "We buy stocks where the near term sucks." Of course, you have to be sure you won't get wiped out by bankruptcy, but Whitman is good at doing just that. In 2008, Third Avenue Value finally met its match and suffered a big loss, while Third Avenue International Value held up nicely. Even so, I have faith in both funds over the long haul.

Because Mr. Whitman is 83, it's good to see that a second generation of managers has proved proficient in running funds in his way. Whitman has said Ian Lapey will take over the flagship Third Avenue Value (TAVFX) when he retires, but he hasn't said when he will retire.

What to Buy: They are all great, but be sure you have a long-term time horizon of 10 years or more before buying.

Vanguard

Vanguard's mutual structure and a laserlike focus on costs mean it is able to offer the lowest expense ratios in almost every case. The firm has great index funds run by skilled managers, of course, but it also has great actively managed funds that are mostly run by outside subadvisors, and bond funds that are run in-house.

Vanguard is about the only fund company where you could build a great portfolio without going outside to another fund company. Because of its cost advantage, Vanguard is able to run funds with lower risk than most and still beat the competition. That's especially true in the bond realm where its funds often take on less credit risk than their peers and still beat them.

Vanguard has proved that it is also a very good selector of active managers. Some of the very best are run by the likes of Wellington, Primecap, and Barrow Hanley. However, in recent years Vanguard has been adding a whole slew of subadvisors to its funds in order to manage inflows. That can be frustrating if you bought the fund just to get the services of one subadvisor. Some funds like Vanguard Explorer have huge rosters of seven or more subadvisors. On the plus side, by allowing more money into the fund, it can reduce taxable capital gains distributions.

What to Buy: If you want to index, start with something that covers a wide swath of the market, like Vanguard Total Stock Market (VTSMX) or even a target-date fund that combines a bunch of index funds. You could also go with Vanguard's tax-managed funds, which do a brilliant job of reducing your tax bill. Be sure to check out the fund's losses in 2000, 2001, 2002, and 2007, because they do, of course, have market risk, and are certain to lose money when the market does.

On the active side, look for those from the best subadvisors I just mentioned. I own two of Vanguard's funds by Primecap (in different accounts).

What to Avoid: Vanguard Florida Long-Term Tax-Exempt (VFLTX) serves no purpose, as Florida doesn't have an income tax. You are sacrificing diversification for nothing.

Wasatch

Founder Sam Stewart adopted what I consider to be the best ownership model: Shares belong to investment professionals and they must sell when they retire. This is a great formula for stability that has worked for American, Dodge & Cox, and other outstanding firms.

Wasatch is a good small-cap shop that has had its ups and downs, but I expect it will rise again. The firm's emphasis on real earnings meant it did amazingly well when the dot-com bubble burst in 2000. It owned more reasonably priced companies, whereas most dot-coms hadn't yet turned a profit and were unreasonably priced in the rare cases where they did. So, while most growth shops were under siege in the bear market of 2000 to 2002, Wasatch was enjoying a big growth spurt. That continued for a while, and it closed most of its funds to new investment.

Then came the boom in oil and other commodities in the wake of the war in Iraq, and Wasatch's fortunes turned sharply. Almost all its resources were focused on traditional growth industries such as technology and healthcare, and Wasatch's performance suffered for it.

Today, Wasatch has a lot of appeal. That growth spurt led it to go on a big hiring spree, yet the subsequent reversal meant it doesn't run a ton of money. Today it has 45 investment professionals and just $9 billion under management. You'd have to look a long time to find another place with that high a ratio of people to assets under management. The firm has used that greater reach to cover more stocks in more industries. It now has value and mid- and large-cap funds, too. Should commodity stocks take a breather, Wasatch funds could be ready to roar. Yet, Wasatch says it will likely close its funds at the same low levels it did last time, so the funds' managers should maintain plenty of maneuverability.

What to Buy: Look for a combination of experienced managers, modest costs, and a strategy close to Wasatch's small-growth knitting. The fund that best fits those criteria is Wasatch Small Cap Growth (WAAEX) run by Jeff Cardon, who is in his twenty-third year at the helm. The fund charges just 1.19 percent, which makes it one of the cheapest in the Wasatch stable.

What to Avoid: Because of their small asset bases, some Wasatch funds are just too pricey. International Opportunities (WAIOX), Micro Cap Value (WAMVX), and Micro Cap (WMICX) all charge more than 2 percent in expenses, so I'd take a pass.

Wellington

In the early 1990s, Fidelity was the envy of the fund industry. In the late 1990s, it was Putnam. But in Boston, they all—including Fidelity and Putnam—wish they were Wellington.

Technically speaking, Wellington isn't a fund company. It is an asset manager that runs money for other fund companies, most prominently Vanguard on the no-load side and Hartford on the load side. Maybe that distance from the sales end of the business is why Wellington has been able to retain its long-term focus. It also helps that it's a partnership where key employees (mostly managers and analysts) own the business.

Wellington has the stability, experience, depth, and abilities that are tough to match. Its funds consistently produce better returns with less risk than the competition. It has seasoned career analysts working with savvy portfolio managers.

You could see the old Putnam in the 1990s trying so hard to look like Wellington with its manager teams and big morning meetings. Only at Putnam it was a veneer to hide a sales-driven culture, whereas Wellington is the real deal. Wellington runs great dependable funds, and it closes them when needed.

What to Buy: Just about everything Wellington does is worth a look. Vanguard's Wellington-run funds are much cheaper than Hartford's. Among the best are two cautious allocation funds: Vanguard Wellington (VWELX) and Vanguard Wellesley Income (VWINX). The former is mostly stock, and the latter is mostly bonds. I also like Vanguard Health Care (VGHCX) run by Ed Owens, who is one of the best sector fund managers around.

9
_____

The Inside Scoop on
Broker-Sold Fund Companies

IN THIS CHAPTER, I, the Fund Spy, am giving you the inside scoop on
the big broker-sold fund companies.

AllianceBernstein

What would happen if you combined a value-oriented disciplined investment firm that serves wealthy clients with a growth-oriented sales driven
mutual fund company? You'd get AllianceBernstein—a company that was
kind of schizophrenic when the merger took effect and one that got in
hot water in the market timing scandal. But fast forward to today, and
Bernstein folks are firmly in charge so that you get lower costs, greater discipline, and funds that do pretty much what they say they're going to do.

The new AllianceBernstein runs some good funds, though none are so exciting that they send my pulse racing.

What to Buy: Conservatively run municipal bond funds like Bernstein New York Municipal are among its best funds. The firm also places great emphasis on complete portfolio solutions, with the idea that investors will fare better when they get a well-balanced, wide-ranging solution. With that in mind, consider AllianceBernstein Balanced Wealth Strategy (ABWAX), which casts a very wide net.

American Funds (a.k.a. Capital Group)

The giant Los Angeles–based firm has a great ownership structure that keeps shares in the hands of employees who have to sell them back after a certain period away from the company. That has helped to keep everyone focused on the long term and to avoid mergers that would mess with the corporate culture.

American has the best model for handling growth in actively managed equity funds, and that's a good thing, because it runs a lot of money and has never closed a fund. Each fund is run by multiple managers who operate independently. In addition, American hands off a big chunk of most funds to the firm's analysts. Rather than close a fund, American will add another manager as assets grow. Because the managers operate independently, they are able to trade in smaller lots and thus avoid having as big an impact on a stock as they would otherwise. You could have two managers buying Merck, one selling, and four more not trading it at all.

The keys to making this system work are depth and patience. American has more extremely bright, experienced investment professionals than just about anyone else. So, when it adds a manager, it can typically call on someone with 10 to 20 years' worth of experience. It also has that kind of experience when it hands off money to the analysts, because American promotes a senior analyst career path equal in pay and stature to portfolio managers. It is also very patient with new analysts, letting them get up to speed over a number of years. Not only does that help analysts to develop, but it also helps to attract them.

The result of all that is that you get huge, wide-ranging portfolios driven by some of the best fundamental research around. The funds aren't nimble, and they more or less have to stick with large-cap stocks for liquidity reasons. But they overcome that with low expense ratios and low turnover.

The one real negative is that American is a bit miserly with disclosure. For example, the firm doesn't tell you how much any individual manager is running, even though that's a key internal consideration when it is deciding where to give new assignments. Technically, the SEC requires that a firm disclose how much a manager is running, but American found a way around that by counting everything in every fund it runs so that you get cartoonish figures of $200 billion and the like, even though any single manager isn't likely to run over $20 billion in total.

What to Buy: American does everything well, which makes its really wide-ranging funds such as world stock, moderate allocation, or world allocation particularly appealing. I'm also a fan of Washington Mutual (AWSHX) (no relation to the failed bank), which has a strict dividend discipline that comes in handy in tough markets. The funds are so wide-ranging that you don't need more than two American domestic-stock funds.

What to Avoid: I like all of American's funds so I won't say there are any you should skip, but I'd say that Smallcap World (SMCWX) and the bond funds are a notch below the rest of the lineup.

Columbia

You know the cartoon showing four fishes with their mouths open as the progressively larger fish is about to swallow the one in front of it? That's how Columbia came into existence. Bank of America, its corporate parent, is the result of scores of mergers, and each bank merger brought a new fund company into the fold. Among those swallowed up were FleetBoston, NationsBank, Liberty Financial, and Wanger Asset Management. By 2003, the picture was rather ugly. Not only did the firm have hundreds of funds, most of which were fairly crummy, but Columbia and its various arms got caught doing a bunch of things it shouldn't in the market-timing scandal.

Since then, Keith Banks and others at Columbia have done a nice job bringing order to the chaos. They chose the best in house for running different strategies and merged similar funds into the good ones. In addition, they've gotten much more rigorous about enforcing ethical and legal compliance so that they don't give shareholders short shrift anymore. Today, performance is much improved and the firm's lineup is decent overall, but not top-tier.

What to Buy: Small-growth boutique Acorn runs some good funds, as does subadvisor Marsico under the Columbia Marsico brand. Probably the best gem of all is David Williams's Columbia Value and Restructuring (UMBIX). Williams is a brilliant stock picker with a long track record of success, though he does most of his own legwork.

What to Avoid: Columbia Asset Allocation (LAAAX) is a messy and pricey grouping of many strategies under one umbrella. It needs greater focus and lower costs.

Davis/Selected

This venerable New York shop is one of the best Buffett-style managers around. It is led by Chris Davis and Ken Feinberg, who are great stewards and patient investors with a strong bias toward financials. That led to some rough returns in 2008, but they still have a great long-term record. Unlike Buffett, they aren't wary of technology. They invest in all sectors but like Buffett they focus on finding great businesses at modest prices.

What to Buy: On the load side, the funds are sold under the Davis name. On the no-load side, it's Selected. The best expression of their work is Davis New York Venture (NYVTX) and its no-load equivalent, Selected American (SLADX). If you buy Selected American, buy directly from the fund firm and you'll get a lower expense ratio.

FPA

Like founder Bob Rodriguez, this firm is ornery and brilliant at the same time. It's a tiny boutique firm run by a few strong-headed value managers. Rodriguez runs a bond fund and a stock fund, and he does a great job at both. His focus on preserving capital means he would gladly let money sit in Treasury bills rather than buy something just for the sake of it. In his great shareholder letters, he regularly rails against manias, investment bankers, and the Federal Reserve. Yet there's a method to his madness. He's usually right when he says prices of a security type don't make sense. When the bond market gets pummeled, his fund is often the only one still in the black. All that protection comes at the cost of missing out on some rallies, but that's a fair price to pay for strong long-term performance with modest risks.

What to Buy: On the load side, there's Bob Rod's FPA Capital (FPPTX) and FPA New Income (FPNIX). In addition, FPA Paramount (FPRAX) is a solid mid-cap fund run by Eric Ende and Steve Geist. On the no-load side, Steve Romick's Crescent Fund (FPACX) is a great balanced fund that's kind of like a tame hedge fund in that Romick will buy almost anything, but he doesn't take on huge risks. Romick was one of the first to say we were in a housing bubble, and his fund was well protected when that bubble burst.

FranklinTempleton

FranklinTempleton is a big believer in specialization. The San Mateo side in California runs bonds and growth stock funds. Bermuda-based Templeton runs international equities, and New Jersey–based Mutual Series runs U.S. value funds (see Mutual Series for separate entry).

That specialization hasn't always led to excellence, though. Franklin's growth funds and Templeton's international funds are decent but not top notch. But Franklin's muni funds and Mutual Series' value funds are outstanding.

What to Buy: Franklin Federal Tax-Free Income (FKTIX) and Franklin High-Yield Tax-Free Income (FRHIX) are excellent aggressive income driven funds. Franklin has the research chops to make its more aggressive muni funds work well.

What to Avoid: Franklin Templeton Founding Funds Allocation (FFALX) is a marketer's dream but a thumb in the eye to investors. Franklin sold the heck out of this fund, but it's really a marketing gimmick. It took three of its oldest funds—Franklin Income, Templeton Growth, and Mutual Shares—and glued them together. Then for some strange but profitable reason, it cranked up the fees so that the combination of the three funds cost more than if you bought them separately. To make things worse, Franklin Income's extreme yield orientation led it to get hit much harder than most allocation funds in 2008 because it held junk bonds and utilities stocks.

MFS

MFS has gone from forgettable to intriguing. For a while it seemed to offer all the blandness of a widely diversified portfolio yet still lag its benchmarks by a wide margin. But a renewed effort to build up its research effort has made MFS quietly intriguing.

It's telling that MFS's two research funds in which analysts pick the stocks directly have been performing well. I take that as a sign that the attempt to build back the analyst staff to its former glory is working.

What to Buy: MFS does a little of everything but most of their top funds seem to be large-cap stock funds. MFS Value (MEIAX), MFS Research (MFRFX), and MFS Core Growth (MFCAX) are all worth a close look.

What to Avoid: Although MFS's stock funds largely acquitted themselves well in the quagmire of 2007 to 2008, MFS High Income (MHITX) got scorched. I'd steer clear of that one. In addition, MFS continues to struggle with small caps, so skip MFS New Discovery (MNDAX).

Mutual Series

Mutual Series is owned by Franklin Templeton, but I'm giving it a separate entry because it is really distinct from the rest of Franklin Templeton. The basic strategy in all the Mutual Series funds is to buy stocks so cheap that there's very little risk. The managers do this in the United States and overseas; they'll even get into *distressed securities,* which are stocks or bonds of companies on the brink of or in bankruptcy.

You wouldn't want to try to do what these folks do, and that's the beauty of it. This research-intensive strategy is tough for the competition to match. In addition, many peers are wary of wading into controversial stocks the way Mutual Series does.

One of the more remarkable things about Mutual Series is that the funds continued to execute their strategies very well even after a number of managers left for hedge funds. The reason is that their experienced analysts stuck around. The firm delegates a lot to analysts, and as long as they're doing their job, it's smooth sailing.

The funds are great ballast for a portfolio. They hold up nicely in most downturns and are less volatile than most.

What to Buy: Any of Mutual Series' funds are good options, but Mutual European (TEMIX) and Mutual Beacon (TEBIX) are among the best.

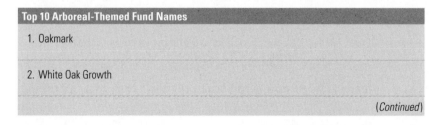

Top 10 Arboreal-Themed Fund Names
1. Oakmark
2. White Oak Growth

(Continued)

3. Oak Value
4. Acorn
5. Evergreen
6. Black Oak Emerging Technology
7. Longleaf
8. Red Oak Technology Select
9. Live Oak Health Sciences
10. Sequoia

Oppenheimer

Oppenheimer is a rather random collection of management teams without many commonalities connecting them. It has a solid but small foreign-stock group that blends top-down and bottom-up investing. The foreign group is running a huge amount of money, given its size. So, my worries are that it will grow too fast or key people will leave.

Oppenheimer also boasts a decent quantitative group that runs U.S.-stock funds under the Main Street name. They're consistent, though unexciting.

Finally, there's the boldest group of all: Oppenheimer's Rochester municipal-bond team. This team takes big risks that generally pay off, except in 2007 and 2008, when a huge weighting in tobacco bonds (bonds linked to states' tobacco settlement revenues) got clobbered. And therein lies the problem. Who wants a muni fund that will earn nice returns in 9 out of 10 years but then lose 15 percent in 1 out of 10? Not many people

I know want to take big chances with muni bonds. They mostly want decent income and no surprises.

What to Buy: International Growth (OIGAX) and Developing Markets (ODMAX) are good picks.

What to Avoid: I'm not a big fan of the muni funds.

Putnam

Although there were many fund companies that got caught doing worse, Putnam was the other public face of the market-timing scandal. Like Janus, Putnam burned investors in the bear market and then got tripped up in the scandal. Unlike Janus, it has been flailing away ever since. The firm has suffered from frequent changes to managers and strategy, departures of managers and analysts, and mostly crappy returns. A few of Putnam's funds have produced respectable returns in recent years, but that's about it. If you want to know why you shouldn't bet on a fund company that's under construction Putnam is exhibit A.

Putnam shows just how hard it is to turn a fund company around when things go bad. You have to convince your best people to stay, convince smart people to come on board, get them all to buy in to the new way of doing things, and then produce good performance quickly before people bolt for firms in better shape. Suffice it to say that despite having cleaned up its ethical problems and having good intentions and deep pockets, Putnam is still a mess.

In fact, its chief investment officer resigned in September 2008 when eight of Putnam's ten largest funds were underperforming over the trailing three-year period. At Putnam, the people change all the time, but the results remain consistently bad.

What to Buy: Nothing.

What to Avoid: Everything.

Top 10 Nautical-Themed Fund Names
1. Vanguard Wellington
2. Clipper
3. RiverSource
4. Sextant Growth
5. Fidelity Magellan
6. Steadman Oceanographic
7. Presidio
8. Harbor
9. Schooner
10. Yacktman

RiverSource

RiverSource was the biggest joke in the fund industry in the 1990s. It did just about everything poorly and had dependably lousy performance. Then, parent company American Express noticed this and also noticed the Ameriprise advisors were losing clients because they had put those clients in crummy in-house funds. American Express opened up its checkbook, hired Ted Truscott, formerly of Scudder, and took on a massive overhaul. It bought some investment boutiques, fired a bunch of managers, raided Fidelity, and generally demanded strong performance from everyone. Today, RiverSource is a respectable shop, although it's not at the top level.

Interesting fact: If you want to get under a fund company's skin, make fun of the new name that they paid a consultant a lot of money to create. I ran a Fund Spy poll to see what readers thought would be a better name than RiverSource: RiverCarp, PondScum, SeaHag, WeHopeYouDon'tRememberWeUsedtoStink, Outflow.

The readers chose PondScum, and Ameriprise/RiverSource blamed me, even though I voted for SeaHag.

Worth a Look: RiverSource Strategic Allocation (IMRFX) is a quant-run allocation fund that's worth a look. In addition bond funds such as RiverSource Diversified Bond are much improved.

What to Avoid: RiverSource's index funds and RiverSource Partners Small Cap Growth A (AXSCX) are too costly to be worth it.

IO

Twenty Great Funds That Passed My Test

Now for the fun part—let's put the pieces together and pick some funds. To see how other funds rate and to see if these funds still measure up, go to the special Web site: www.morningstar.com/goto/fundspy.

Criteria for Fund Selection

I looked for funds that:

▶ Have manager investment of $500,000 or more. (See Chapter 2.)
▶ Have low trading costs. (See Chapter 3.)

- ▶ Have expense ratios in the cheapest quintile in their category. (See Chapter 4.)
- ▶ Have long-term returns dating back to the longest-tenured manager's start date that beat the fund's benchmark. (See Chapter 5.)
- ▶ Have sound strategies and reasonable risks. (See Chapter 6.)
- ▶ Do not have poor stewardship grades of C or lower. (See Chapter 7.)
- ▶ Have outstanding managers. (See Chapters 7, 8, and 9.)

We don't have trading cost data for bond funds or international funds, so I left trading costs out of the equation for them. For index funds, all that really matters is expenses, trading costs, and diversification, so I left everything else out for them.

Twenty Great Funds

Here, then, are 20 funds that pass the test. Below, I'll let you know what the competitive advantages are. To shed more light on these 20 funds, go to Appendix B where we feature data tables, highlighting fees, management information, and past performance.

Large-Cap U.S. Stock

1. **American Funds Fundamental Investors (ANCFX)**—This fund brings together a number of outstanding managers at American. Each operates independently, but they all invest in large-cap stocks based on fundamental factors. The fund has produced outstanding long-term returns.

   Competitive Advantages: Depth—The number of excellent, experienced managers and analysts at this fund is its greatest strength. You can buy the fund and put it away because you don't have to worry about one manager retiring. Costs—This fund's expense ratio is one of the lowest you'll find at an actively managed, broker-sold fund.

2. **Fidelity Spartan Total Market Index (FSTMX)**—Fidelity is undercutting the competition with an expense ratio of 0.10 percent, making it the cheapest fund available to the average investor.

    Competitive Advantage: Costs.

3. **T. Rowe Price Equity Income (PRFDX)**—I love funds with a dividend focus like this one. It gives the fund downside protection while delivering a nice stream of income, even in rough markets. Manager Brian Rogers is an unflappable value investor who never loses sight of the importance of protecting against losses.

    Competitive Advantages: Rogers's experience and T. Rowe's analyst staff are a great combination.

4. **T. Rowe Price New America Growth (PRWAX)**—Joe Milano is one of the next generation of managers at T. Rowe. He has 6 years at the helm, and I can imagine Milano sticking around for 20 more. He looks for low-debt, high-growth companies trading at reasonable prices. Tellingly, the fund's best year of relative performance was 2008 (through October), when the market and highly leveraged companies, in particular, were getting pummeled.

    Competitive Advantages: The fund's small asset base, T. Rowe's growth analysts, and Milano's steady hand.

5. **Vanguard Primecap Core (VPCCX)**—This fund's close relative, the closed Vanguard Primecap, actually passed the performance test, while this fund's record is too short. However, both funds are run in a similar fashion, so I included still-open Primecap Core instead. Both are large-growth funds, although this one has a heavier emphasis on cyclical growth. It's one of the best growth funds around. Primecap is a deep-growth shop, and its managers' strategy has been proven over the long haul.

    Competitive Advantage: An experienced staff of analysts and managers allows it to go deeper than most growth managers. While many competitors are investing based on momentum and buzz, Primecap is focused on the fundamentals.

Mid- and Small-Cap U.S. Stock

6. **FPA Capital (FPPTX)**—This stock fund is focused on preserving capital while still earning strong long-term returns. Manager Bob Rodriguez will happily sit out a rally if he doesn't see anything attractive. Usually, the market comes back to him under those circumstances. He was one of the first to sound alarm bells about the subprime mess.

   Competitive Advantages: Rodriguez is a savvy investor whose approach is too difficult and too uncorporate to have many imitators. The fund is also very reasonably priced.

7. **Janus Midcap Value (JMCVX)**—This a great straightforward value fund run for Janus by Perkins, Wolf, McDonnell & Co. The managers look for companies with depressed shares but clean balance sheets so that they can get back on their feet. It has worked brilliantly for 10 years.

   Competitive Advantages: Their long-term focus and knowledge of these companies from when they were small caps has enabled managers Tom Perkins and Jeff Kautz to make great stock picks.

8. **T. Rowe Price Small Value (PRSVX)**—Manager Preston Athey runs a cautious, diversified fund very much in the T. Rowe mode. There are no big bets; the fund just quietly plugs along and earns strong returns.

   Competitive Advantages: Athey is a very experienced manager, supported by sharp small-cap analysts. In addition, T. Rowe has helped to preserve returns in the past by closing the fund when needed.

Allocation

9. **American Funds Capital Income Builder (CAIBX)**—This fund covers a lot of ground, and it does it well. It has foreign and domestic stocks, and a quarter of its assets are in bonds. If you want to simplify things, this is a great way to do it. You get tremendous diversification

but you still get strong active management. Another way to look at it is that it's a very mild way to get exposure to overseas markets.

Competitive Advantages: Same as for American Funds Fundamental Investors (see page 112).

10. **Dodge & Cox Balanced (DODBX)**—This is a great conservative way to invest. Dodge's bond team is as good as its stock team so when you stick the two together you get a great balanced fund. It's boring but quite effective over the long haul.

Competitive Advantages: Stability—Most of Dodge's analysts and managers stay for a whole career. Depth—Dodge has a deep bench. Low costs—Dodge stays out of fund supermarkets in order to keep costs low. Focus—Dodge runs only five mutual funds, and they are based on just three portfolios: U.S. stocks, foreign stocks, and fixed income.

11. **Vanguard Wellington (VWELX)**—A brilliant conservative fund. The fund has about two thirds of assets in a large-cap value strategy and one third in fixed income. Wellington has proved adept in both arenas. This is a good fund if you're looking to take a bit of the edge off the market's extremes.

Competitive Advantages: A deep team focused on the long term. Wellington attracts outstanding analysts and managers. In addition, Vanguard's cost controls help make this one of the cheapest actively managed balanced funds around.

International Stock

12. **Columbia Acorn International (ACINX)**—Small-cap growth investing overseas can get pretty crazy, but Zach Egan and Louis Mendes bring a welcome, sober approach. They look for healthy companies with strong fundamentals where the stock is trading for a modest price. They're patient, too—the fund's turnover is well below 50 percent a year.

Competitive Advantages: Low costs and solid fundamental underpinning.

13. **Dodge & Cox International (DODFX)**—This fund is still ahead of its benchmark after a harsh 2008. Every strategy has its weaknesses, and the shortcomings of Dodge's value strategy were revealed in 2008. However, all of the fundamentals remain in place. It's a handy, though unwelcome, illustration of my point that you should sell on failing fundamentals and not short-term performance. Led by Diana Strandberg, the fund seeks out well-run companies trading at a discount. Although Dodge & Cox is a conservative firm, the fund isn't shy about investing in emerging markets.

Competitive Advantages: Same as for Dodge & Cox Balanced (see page 115).

14. **Matthews Pacific Tiger (MAPTX)**—Matthews's managers are Asia specialists who try to take some of the risk out of investing in emerging markets. Mind you, that means when Asia is down 40 percent, this fund might be down 35 percent, so it's not a low-risk fund. Still, Matthews has built up a great analyst staff dedicated to Asia.

Competitive Advantages: No one can match Matthews's Asia staff. The fund also charges fairly low costs, by emerging-markets fund standards.

15. **Vanguard International Value (VTRIX)**—Who says investing overseas has to be pricey? Vanguard has assembled four excellent subadvisors to run this fund all for just 0.40 percent. Because you have four managers, the fund is a blend of different value strategies, and that leads to smoother performance. Hansberger Global Partners is the longest-serving of the four subadvisors, and the fund has been a standout since it came on board in 2000.

Competitive Advantages: Skilled experienced subadvisors; Vanguard is skilled in picking managers and switching if needed; it holds down costs.

Bonds

16. **Fidelity Muni Income (FHIGX)**—Fidelity's municipal-bond group is one of the best around, and it shows in the returns of this fund and others. Fidelity has built up a great team of managers, quantitative analysts, and traders in its muni group. They take a bunch of little bets based on individual issue and quantitative analysis. In general, that leads to consistent outperformance.

    Competitive Advantages: Research—Municipal-bond teams tend to be smaller than taxable-bond teams, but Fidelity really has built out its team nicely so that you get the benefit of tremendous resources. Costs—Only Vanguard has cheaper muni funds.

17. **Harbor Bond (HABDX)**—Want to put arguably the best bond-fund manager from arguably the best bond firm to work for you? Of course you do. This gem is run by Bill Gross and PIMCO, who have an uncanny knack for staying ahead of the market. This fund's returns are absolutely amazing.

    Competitive Advantages: PIMCO has built up an outstanding group of managers, analysts, quants, and traders to run enormous sums of money. Their scale and influence give them an edge others can't match.

18. **TCW Total Return Bond (TGLMX)**—This is a mortgage-focused fund that actually thrived amid the subprime mess of 2007 and 2008. Managers Jeffrey Gundlach and Philip Barach saw the subprime mess coming and stuck to the most dependable slices of the mortgage market. That kept the fund in the black in both years. I figure any fund that can withstand that mess can take just about anything.

    Competitive Advantages: TCW's mortgage expertise and this fund's low costs make it a winner.

19. **Vanguard Inflation Protected Securities (VIPSX)**—TIPS, or Treasury Inflation-Protected Securities, are a unique security type that pays you

more when inflation rises, whereas most bond funds lose value when inflation rises. So if you have a lot of your portfolio in fixed income, TIPS are a valuable diversifier. And Vanguard's low costs make its funds a natural choice when you buy high-quality bonds.

Competitive Advantage: Costs.

20. **Vanguard Total Bond Index (VBMFX)**—What's so great about matching a bond index after a low expense ratio? Well, in the bond world, the higher the expense ratio, the greater the likelihood a manager will take big risks to produce a competitive yield. So, this fund doesn't just offer you nice returns when things are going well in the bond market. It also has less risk, and that's a big comfort when the bond world is up in arms.

Competitive Advantage: Costs.

Conclusion

Investing is really about putting the odds in your favor. You can't guarantee a good outcome, but by combining the most important factors in mutual fund success, I've built a list of funds where the odds are strongly in their favor.

As I look at the list, one thing that stands out is stability. Most of these funds have tremendous support and come from fund companies with few manager departures. To be sure, I'd consider selling if many managers from these firms left or if costs surged unexpectedly. True, FPA Capital is all about the manager, and I'd consider selling it if Bob Rodriguez left, but most of these funds have enough team support so that shouldn't be much of an issue.

I'll keep you posted about how these funds rate, as well as other funds on the Fund Spy Web page www.morningstar.com/goto/fundspy. Please check it out to get the latest. I'll even tweak the formula if new studies suggest adjusting the weightings or adding new data points.

If there's one thing that unites nearly all the great investors it's that they keep things simple and they remain patient. If you build a good investment plan and choose great funds, you'll see just how powerful a formula it can be. Just don't pop the cake out of the oven before it's done. Be patient, and watch your funds with their competitive advantages in mind. As long as those advantages remain in place, you're on the right path.

Appendix A

The Best of Eleven Years of Fund Spies

I CAN'T BELIEVE I have been writing the Fund Spy column on Morningstar.com for 11 years. I've been covering the fund industry in sickness and health. Through genius and silliness. Through scandal and acclaim.

What follows are some of my favorite columns. Should you wonder what happens to marketing-driven trend-chasers, consider my 1997 column on Strong Funds. It was six years before Strong would get in trouble with Eliot Spitzer, and three years before it would launch an Internet Fund in March 2000—yes, Strong nailed the top of the market precisely.

As a hater of trendy funds, I'll admit to taking a little joy in Internet funds' demise. Of those I wrote about in the fourth column here, only

Jacob Internet is still around, though not in a way that's very profitable for investors.

Let the record show that I once made a smart call on the market. I warned investors not to pass up value funds in March 2000. No, I had no clue that that was the moment the bubble would burst. I just knew that markets rotate and that a contrarian approach and a diversified portfolio will keep you out of the worst excesses of Wall Street.

I've also had the chance to talk with some of the great investors of our age, including Marty Whitman. Whitman is a cantankerous but fun value investor who hates trendy investments and doesn't care what conventional wisdom says.

Sometimes, my Fund Spy column is a stump for speechifying. I used the column to campaign for disclosure of manager investments. It struck me as unfair that CEOs of publicly traded companies had to spell out how much of company stock they owned but fund managers didn't have to disclose their investments in their own funds. Not long after, the SEC decided to require manager investment disclosure, which makes up a key component of our research process today (see Chapter 2).

Then there's the matter of a couple of bets. Fund of funds manager Bob Markman has bet Jack Bogle that he could overcome his sizable fee handicap through fund trading to beat Vanguard 500. He has lost that bet twice.

My column on fund size was a precursor to our work on trading costs. When a fund gets too big, its trading costs may surge. Now we have the data to track when a fund's trading costs surge.

Also, I offer up a before and after look at someone who has made brilliant market calls. Jeremy Grantham said in 2007 that investors should wring out the risks in their portfolio in anticipation of a big sell-off. Sure enough, it happened, and when it got to its worst point in October 2008, Grantham was ready with a lot of dry powder to start buying stocks at super low prices.

Strong Funds' Marketing Department— A Contrarian Indicator

Fund Spy | By Russel Kinnel | 09-23-97 | 12:00 AM | This article originally appeared on Morningstar.com.

Make that a great contrarian indicator. In the first half of 1996, IPO stocks were hotter than the sun. Funds that bought them by the bushel had run up huge gains. By the summer of 1996, Strong Funds leapt into action and hired Mary Lisanti, the champion IPO manager, away from Bankers Trust. That moment marked the peak for IPO mania and the next nine months proved brutal for Strong Small Cap, which lost 19%.

When the fizz went out of IPOs, market leadership returned to the titans such as General Electric and Microsoft. As a result, S&P 500 Index funds looked great, and about the only actively managed funds to beat them were betting even more on the biggest stocks. (Picture a light bulb going on over the head of someone at Strong.) "Why not index just the 100 largest stocks in half a fund's portfolio and give a manager the ability to double her bets on some of those stocks in the other half?" And so, Strong Blue Chip 100 was born. The fund came out at the end of June, just in time for the long-awaited revival of small caps. In July and August, small caps as measured by the Russell 2000 returned a healthy 7.05% while the S&P 100 returned a mere 1.2%.

What Strong Funds really should do is save the hassle of coming out with a new gimmick every year and instead introduce the Strong Shameless Trend-Hopping Fund. Strong could give the fund a wide charter to invest in whatever earned the biggest returns in the past month.

Planned Obsolescence

Speaking of gimmicks, the HomeState Year 2000 Fund is due to be rolled out in a month, promising to invest in companies that will make money by solving the most brazen example of human stupidity, the Year 2000 bug. To steal a line from Dave Barry, we are not making this up. It would have been a nifty idea three years ago when companies and investors were just waking up to the scope of the problem. But now? These stocks have already gone up by huge amounts, yet there's no certainty what will happen to them in 2001. The managers note that they can also buy established businesses like IBM and Oracle that will certainly be around after the year 2000, but it's not like those firms will be getting most of their revenues from Year 2000 solutions. If HomeState can come out with a Year 2000 fund at the end of 1997, then someone else should come out with the Operating System Fund based on the premise that those fellas up in Redmond might be on to something.

Fidelity Average-Priced Stock Fund

When Fidelity Low-Priced Stock Fund was introduced with a $10 price limit on the shares it could buy, it sounded kind of gimmicky, but the results indicated otherwise. That screen led manager Joel Tillinghast to invest in obscure small-value stocks and the fund earned outstanding returns with very little risk. Of course, a strong-performing Fidelity fund always attracts a crowd. That effect was magnified because Low-Priced Stock was one of only two small-cap options from Fidelity, and the other one was the mediocre quantitative Fidelity Small Cap Fund. In just 7 years, Low-Priced Stock has swelled to $9 billion in assets, an absurd size for a small-cap value fund.

To accommodate that girth, Fidelity has raised the price limit a couple of times, most recently to $35. The move is understandable because the giant asset base forced Tillinghast to hold a lot in cash, even though the fund owned 900 stocks. In fact, the asset base is so restrictive that the fund holds more than 100 positions that account for a mere 0.01% of assets each.

Still, it's a shame that Fidelity had to abandon some of this fund's character. It can now buy such giants as RJR Nabisco and Pharmacia & Upjohn. However, most of this fund's success is attributable to the fact that it is about the only outlet for all of Fidelity's analysts' small-cap picks. Unfortunately, that's also the reason Fidelity has refused to close it. Fidelity needs a good small-cap offering as part of its 401(k) lineup and this is the only option. From shareholders' standpoint, closing the fund is a better option than raising the minimum price, but Fidelity doesn't want to give up on billions of dollars in 401(k) assets.

Don't Miss the Next Value Rally

Fund Spy | By Russel Kinnel | 03-21-00 | 12:00 AM | This article originally appeared on Morningstar.com.

Market-timers learn a costly lesson.

When we Morningstarites talk about value, individual investors often tell us, "That sounds great. I'm not going to buy a value fund now, though, because I can move in there when the rally starts."

I guess they figure that all rallies work out like the technology rally of the past couple of years. Graph Nasdaq's returns, and you get something that looks like a trip up Mount Everest. So what if you missed the first leg? There's still a few hundred percentage points left in the rally.

It's pretty rare that it works that way, unfortunately. You've got to endure the dismal stretches to get the good stuff. Value companies are way too cyclical for a nice smooth line. Remember the second quarter of 1999? Grungy industries were in vogue, and the papers were filled with stories about people switching into value and what basic industries were the most attractive. If you had switched from growth to value, you would have missed out on one of the great tech rallies in history, and you would have moved in just in time to get pummeled, because value swooned. There's no way to know whether last week's rally was the start of something big or just a fake to cost the market-timers more money.

In the long run, market-timing can cost you dearly. I dug up some data going back to 1979 to prove my point. From January 1979 to February 2000, the Russell 1000 Value index returned 2,301%. But if you had missed the best month, you would have cut 300 percentage points off that for a return of 2,013%. Had you missed the best three-month period, you would have shaved more than 500 percentage points off your return, for a return of 1,788%. Rallies and sell-offs have the annoying trait of being unpredictable. The best I can do is to be diversified and patient.

An Oddball Fund with Great Results

Fund Spy | By Russel Kinnel | 08-29-00 | 06:00 AM | This article originally appeared on Morningstar.com.

Marty Whitman does it his way

A few years ago I was chatting with superplanner Harold Evensky and I raised the subject of one of my favorite funds: Third Avenue Value TAVFX). "I've never figured out what's so wonderful about (Third Avenue Value comanager) Marty Whitman," Evensky said. "He hasn't beaten DFA U.S. Large Cap Value DFLVX." That was certainly true back when he said it, but it wasn't the best benchmark.

I can understand why Third Avenue Value isn't that popular with the planning set. It's tough to fit it snugly into a portfolio because it ventures into a whole slew of asset classes. A fund would have to be remarkable to justify putting such an unwieldy investment in a client's portfolio. It has typically had a majority of assets in small-cap stocks but also a chunk in mid- and large caps. From time to time it has held bonds, Japanese stocks, and rather illiquid debt of companies on the ropes. No single benchmark really fits this fund.

Betting against someone as knowledgeable as Evensky isn't a very smart idea, but what the heck—I think I can make a case for this fund. For a benchmark to measure the fund's record, I'll take a matrix approach. The fund has some mid-value stocks, some large-value stocks, and some growth stocks, so let's compare it with a bunch of fund category averages. Since its 1990 inception through last week, Third Avenue Value has returned an annualized 20.11%, which is well ahead of the three

value categories that had average returns between 15.9% and 16.2%. (Yes, it's also ahead of DFA U.S. Large Value by about 2.5 percentage points.) It's also worthwhile to compare the fund with small blend, because it has owned semiconductor stocks and some other tech issues when they were severely out of favor. Small blend returned 17% over that time. Only the S&P 500—not a great benchmark for a fund with a median market cap of $1.2 billion—beat Third Avenue Value, and that was by just 20 basis points.

That's great, but only if Whitman isn't taking on wacky risks. The good news is that he isn't. Whitman is one of the more risk-conscious guys around, and it shows in the fund's results. It actually has one of the lowest standard deviations in the small-value universe as well as the broader domestic-stock fund world.

I'd say Marty's onto something. He's got a sound strategy that few people have been able to copy, and this is why the fund will be worth holding even when DFA Large Value swings ahead of it at some later date. He rejects both classic growth and Graham and Dodd value strategies in favor of an approach that says you should buy a business for far less than the price it's trading for. This means finding businesses that are hated by the markets and determining what they're worth even if almost everything goes wrong. For example, he bought semiconductor stocks when there was a chip glut and Japanese insurers when the value of their holdings collapsed. The first bet was a huge winner and the second one a mistake; yet Whitman was close enough with the insurers that they didn't wipe out the chipmakers' gains.

I guess the lesson here is that when you find a manager who does something very well and it's very hard to imitate, you gotta buy and hold.

Dot-Com Dead Pool for Funds

Fund Spy | By Russel Kinnel | 04-02-01 | 06:00 AM | This article originally appeared on Morningstar.com.

Last year's sudden market reversal spells doom for lots of new funds. Start off with a loss and it will take years to produce a good record and that means years of losing money running a mutual fund. New fund performance has actually been much worse than the S&P 500 because so many were launched to hop on the hottest spots of the market like Internet and biotech.

Of the domestic-stock funds launched in 1999, a hefty 38% are in the red since their launch date. For funds born in 2000, 83% of stock funds have lost money. What this means is a lot of funds won't make it to 2002. Already, Zero Gravity Internet and the Internet Index have folded. Here, then, is a look at some of the biggest money-losers and their odds of survival.

Potomac Internet Plus

As of March 27, this fund has lost 83% since its inception in December 1999 and it's down to just $4 million in assets. No one will fault the manager—it's a leveraged index fund—but will anyone be enthusiastic enough to buy a leveraged net fund? Potomac has over $200 million in assets, so it could probably keep this fund running if it wanted to. I'll give it a 60% chance of surviving the year and a 100% chance of being mentioned as a sign of irrational exuberance.

Jacob Internet JAMFX

This fund is off a stunning 83% since inception.

Ryan Jacob was an Internet hero for the huge returns he produced at the Internet Fund. Now he's down to his last $24 million and he doesn't have other funds to cushion the blow like Potomac does. I give this one an 80% chance of survival because Jacob will probably hope he'll be able to cash in on his fame again.

Westcott Technology NETAX

It began as Westcott Nothing But Net and it has the Internet-like returns to prove it. This tiny fund is off 72% since inception and has less than $1 million in assets. Odds of survival: 0.1%.

Merrill Lynch Internet Strategy MBNTX

Though it's down 71% since inception, the fund still has over $300 million in assets. Obviously, that's plenty of money to pay the bills. However, Merrill swept the awful record of Merrill Lynch Tech under the rug by merging it with Merrill Lynch Global Tech MAGTX) and it might want to do the same with this one. I give it a 50-50 chance.

Strong Internet SNETX

This fund is down 63% and it still has $34 million left. I give it a good chance of survival. However, if it continues to go down, I wouldn't be surprised to see it get a name change or merge into Strong's tech fund.

Genomicsfund.com GENEX

The name says it all doesn't it? This fund hasn't lost

as much as its peers. It's only down 50% over the past 12 months. Still, it already sounds dated. I bet it will see 2002, but that might be about the end.

Fund Firms Were Duped by Enron

Fund Spy | By Russel Kinnel | 12-10-01 | 06:00 AM | This article originally appeared on Morningstar.com.

By now you've probably read which mutual funds got caught holding Enron (ENE) in November. In fact, very few funds had any meaningful exposure by the time Enron completed its dramatic meltdown a couple weeks ago.

While the majority of fund managers missed the last act, most were still players in the drama. Enron was a very popular pick not too long ago. When it fell from $80 to $10 over the course of a few months, it singed scores of funds just as it burned lots of individual investors and pension funds.

I'm willing to give the funds a pass on some of the blame. When earnings are misstated and important bits of information are kept out of sight, it's tough for even the most diligent investor to smell something fishy.

However, I'm amazed at how much buyers of Enron shares were willing to pay for mere trading profits. That's what fund managers—and anyone else who bought Enron—should be embarrassed about.

Historically, Wall Street has placed a very low multiple on trading profits because they're not easy to repeat. Back when Salomon Brothers and Lehman were publicly traded companies, the Street would place a multiple of between 6 and 10 on their trading profits. Yet, Enron's trading profits were valued at huge multiples as though energy trading were somehow different than bond trading.

My guess is that when those trading profits come from one of the few big companies posting sizable earnings growth, a lot of growth managers are willing to suspend their disbelief and hop on board.

I took a look at which fund companies bought when Enron was near its peak between October 2000 and February 2001. Nearly every big fund family made the list. Fidelity, Vanguard, AIM, Putnam, Janus, AXP, Alliance, Oppenheimer, and Merrill Lynch all had funds that bought Enron then. Alliance Premier Growth (APGAX) bought 3.2 million shares in the fourth quarter of 2000. AXP New Dimensions (INNDX) bought 2.4 million and Vanguard U.S. Growth (VWUSX) bought 1.6 million.

A total of 15 funds had 5% of assets or more riding on Enron in the first quarter and you have to wonder what made them so comfortable with that kind of bet. The biggest bet was made by utility index fund Galaxy II Utility Index (IUTLX), which had 11.98% of assets in Enron. You can't blame them for matching their index, but rest of the big betters don't have that excuse. The 10 biggest Enron weightings after Galaxy II Utility are listed below.

8.34% AIM Global Infrastructure (GIFAX)

6.82% Fidelity Select Energy (FSENX)

6.79% Fidelity Advisor Natural Resources (FAGNX)

6.30% Dessauer Global Equity (DGLEX)

6.27% Fidelity Select Natural Gas (FSNGX)

6.18% PIMCO Select Growth (PSGRX)

6.27% Fidelity Select Natural Resources (FNARX)

5.76% Galaxy Large Cap Growth (GALVX)

5.54% The Water Fund M$-DEIF

5.16% Midas Special Equities (MISEX)

Not every fund shop got taken in. American Funds wasn't among those buying lots of shares. Interestingly, they were burned less by the Internet sell-off, too. American is a rigorous stock researcher and they pay more attention to valuations than the typical shop.

All managers make mistakes—though it's rare that they're as big as Enron. The smart ones will at least learn from this expensive lesson and avoid buying future Enrons.

How Much Does Your Fund Manager Haul In?

Fund Spy | By Russel Kinnel | 01-27-03 | 06:00 AM | This article originally appeared on Morningstar.com.

Do you have a right to know how your manager is compensated?

Now that the Securities and Exchange Commission has decided to require disclosure of fund company proxy votes, it's time to get down to the good stuff. Proxy disclosure is an entitlement of shareholders, but there are more important things that will directly impact fund investors' bottom line. In this column and the next we'll discuss two areas that I hope the SEC will roll up their sleeves and get to work on. Of course, the fund industry could get ahead of this issue so that the SEC doesn't. Had the Investment Company Institute, the mutual fund industry trade group, come out with its proxy disclosure proposal soon after the Enron debacle, I doubt the SEC would have adopted its more comprehensive rules. I slightly prefer the rules the SEC came up with, but obviously the ICI doesn't.

Greater Disclosure of Manager Incentives

A manager's incentives tell you a lot about how a fund will be run. How so? A manager whose bonus is tied to 12-month returns will run his fund differently from a manager whose bonus is tied to three-year returns. Likewise, one whose incentive is based on pretax returns will naturally pay little heed to aftertax returns. A manager compensated for asset growth is less likely to push to close his fund.

If you own a stock, you can learn what the CEO is paid, how many shares she owns, what her bonus is based on, and how her option package works. Morningstar director of stock analysis Pat Dorsey has written some good pieces on just how valuable this information is for a stock investor. The SEC decided long ago that this is material information for a stock investor and you can be sure that fund managers scour that information closely. So, I'd like to see the same thing for funds.

I don't even need to know what managers' salaries are. Just tell me what percent of their salary they can earn in their bonus. Then tell me how all the mechanisms in their incentive package work. Finally, I want to know how much money they have in their funds. When managers believe in their funds, they tend to invest quite a lot. If they don't, however, then that's a valuable signal to stay away. For instance, this information is required with closed-end funds and we saw some trendy funds that invested in Russia and Vietnam where the managers hadn't invested a penny. This information might have spared some unfortunate investors in Internet Funds. In addition, a manager who can earn more in his bonus than he has invested in his fund is likely to be a bigger risk-taker.

Further, we've seen that fund managers with truly large sums of money in their funds tend to act as stewards of capital. They're loath to suffer absolute losses, they focus on the long term, and they try to minimize the tax bill because they'll get hit with a bigger bill than any of their shareholders.

Some in the fund industry have said that revealing how much a manager has in his fund would confuse investors. "You wouldn't expect a manager of a short-term bond fund to have all his money in it, would you?" they ask. Of course not. Someone who bothers to look at this figure no doubt is aware that there's a difference between core funds and peripheral funds. I wouldn't expect a manager of a short-term bond fund to have all of his money at stake, but I would expect him to have something in the fund.

In its fight over the proxy issue, the ICI mailed out phone-book-sized documents to illustrate how onerous the rules would be. You could fit all the manager disclosure information I'm calling for on a post card.

Bogle Beats Markman in a Rout

Fund Spy | By Russel Kinnel | 05-29-03 | 06:00 AM | This article originally appeared on Morningstar.com.

Bob Markman loses $25, bragging rights

It seems like just yesterday, but it was really a little more than five years ago. Back in 1995, Bob Markman bet on his fund-picking skills against Jack Bogle's indexing skills. Specifically, Markman bet Bogle $25 (a big sum for a cheapskate like Bogle) that Markman Moderate Allocation MMMGX) could whip Vanguard 500 Index VFINX) over the next five years.

It wasn't much of a horse race. It was over almost as soon as they left the chutes. In 1996, Markman Moderate's 11% return was a little less than half Vanguard 500's. In 1997, Vanguard 500 won 33% to 19%. After five years like that, Vanguard 500 won 226.4% to 156.4%. Ouch. Last week, Markman paid up. (Bonus points to our own John Rekenthaler, who told The New York Times back then that he would bet on Bogle.)

Markman argues that his fund's diversification put him at a disadvantage and takes solace in knowing that his funds earned better returns than their Vanguard LifeStrategy counterparts. Bogle will have none of it. "The fact of the matter is that both the Markman Moderate Portfolio and the Vanguard Index 500 Portfolio took risks that were virtually identical, with respective standard deviations of 14.0% and 14.7%. Thus, our Index Fund's risk-adjusted return (Sharpe ratio) of 1.47 was fully 31% higher than your ratio of 1.12," he argues in a letter to Markman. Bogle goes on to point out that Vanguard 500 won by more than 100 percentage points if you factor in taxes.

Bogle also jumps all over Markman's claim that he takes solace in the fact that his funds outperfomed Vanguard's LifeStrategy funds and most other funds of funds. Referring to funds of funds that charge an extra layer of fees, he says "Being the best of a breed of losers, it seems to me, shouldn't entitle you to bragging rights." He points out that LifeStrategy funds have better Sharpe ratios than their counterparts at Markman, so I guess both can claim a moral victory.

A New Bet

Bogle even offers to renew the bet for $5 over five years. "We'll continue to use Vanguard 500 Index, and you can pick any of your funds you wish…. But if you want to forget the Moderate Portfolio, I think, in fairness, we ought to use the risk-adjusted returns as the fair comparison."

Like John Rekenthaler, I'll put my money on Jack.

Grantham: Stocks Haven't Been This Cheap since 1987

Fund Spy | By Russel Kinnel | 10-14-04 | 06:00 AM | This article originally appeared on Morningstar.com.

Market seer Jeremy Grantham predicted financial debacle, and now he's buying.

A couple weeks ago I had a scary thought: Things are worse than Jeremy Grantham predicted. It's kind of frightening when one of the most bearish market seers has understated the risks and intriguing at the same time because he was really on the money. So, I checked in with him on Monday, Oct. 13 to see what he makes of the current situation. The markets were up about 5% when we spoke, and Grantham thought it had come close to returning to fair value.

Back in July 2007, I spoke with Grantham, who predicted half of the hedge funds and at least one major U.S. bank would be wiped out. Grantham is chairman of asset manager GMO LLC, which runs mutual funds and hedge funds. He advocated going into all manner of anti-risk baskets such as Treasury bills and TIPS as a way of preserving capital while waiting for markets to get cheaper. Back then he sounded like a prophet of doom, but now he just sounds like a prophet. In fact, his firm, GMO, got its 10-year predictions for returns on the S&P 500 and emerging markets for the period ended third quarter 2008 almost exactly right.

In July 2007, Grantham warned of a financial bubble as hedge funds, private equity, and homeowners gorged on debt.

Today Grantham says we're in for slowing global economic growth. In particular, he believes China will slow down more than expected as most economists have taken in their forecasts for Chinese growth only a touch. He argues that China is very dependent upon exports and that the countries on the other end of the trade are too weak.

Grantham expects that slowing growth will also keep commodity prices falling. "I would keep out of commodities for the near term," he said.

In addition, he sees the deleveraging—an unpleasant unwinding of debt—leading to a reverse wealth effect for companies and consumers alike. Both had been living beyond their means and now will have to adjust to below-average earnings and income, and that means they'll be tight with spending.

Nonetheless he's now more constructive about equities because he believes they are trading at severely depressed prices. He said that at the end of Friday, global equities were trading as cheaply as they had been since the 1980s. In fact, the U.S. had traded below GMO's fair value estimate—though as we spoke Monday morning a rally had brought it back to around fair value. Specifically, he prefers blue chips to small caps or highly leveraged companies.

"We're buying carefully and slowly," Grantham notes. Why slowly? "When bubbles correct, they usually overcorrect so that the market is selling well below fair value."

Interestingly Grantham also says he's now neutral on financials—a sector he has long disliked. He notes that most of the credit crisis is likely behind us and that the newest plan of worldwide governments to inject capital into banks in exchange for shares is a big improvement on past plans.

So, add Grantham to the list of sage investors who see this as a huge buying opportunity. The list includes Marty Whitman and Dan Fuss .

Is Your Fund Too Fat?

Fund Spy | By Russel Kinnel | 11-01-04 | 06:00 AM | This article originally appeared on Morningstar.com.

How to tell when asset size could begin hurting your returns

What is a fund's optimal asset size, and when do assets grow so large that a fund's girth hurts its performance?

Growth in asset level beyond a certain point causes a fund problems because it can raise trading costs or force management to change its investment strategy to accommodate the bigger asset base. In addition, rapid growth can overwhelm management's abilities to find attractive investments. For instance, Longleaf Partners LLPFX closed to new investors this summer to avoid ending up in the situation that Aegis Value AVALX is in, with more than half its portfolio sitting in cash.

I've tried to answer the questions posed above in a couple of ways in the pages of Morningstar FundInvestor. I found that you can get a handle on whether a fund's size is a problem by looking at turnover ratios and the amount of daily trading volume that a fund's portfolio holdings soak up. I also found that it was telling to examine a fund's asset level compared with that of its category rivals.

Those are pretty involved ways of divining when a fund is past its ideal asset level. However, there's another rather simple way to look at it. Ask the fund managers.

Hundreds of fund managers have closed their portfolios to new investment. In fact, about half of the assets in small-cap funds are in closed funds. If asset size weren't a problem, fund managers would never close their funds. After all, if it's not hurting performance, any fund company would rather let one of its funds keep growing and collect the additional fees that would come with running more money. If anything, most fund companies are going to err on the side of managing too much rather than too little because closing funds hurts near-term profitability. (On the other hand, it can be argued that fund closings help long-term profitability because investors judge fund companies by their track record and how much money the funds have made for them.)

Many shareholder-friendly fund companies give a lot of thought to how much money they can manage effectively. Some managers, like John Bogle Jr., set a target closing level even before their funds have launched. You can find some views on the subject at the Web sites of Turner Funds and Dodge & Cox. Naturally, no one has a better handle on a fund's capabilities than management. That doesn't always mean they'll close a fund on time, of course. Until Bob Pozen took over Fidelity, the company steadfastly refused to close funds despite mounting evidence that it was hurting returns.

So, to get an idea of what fund managers think is an optimal size, I looked at the total asset levels at all the closed funds in our database at the time of their closing. I found the figures for 83 funds and grouped them by market cap. For each group, I calculated the median asset size at time of closing to come up with a consensus closing level. In large caps the median was $18 billion, in mid-caps it was $3 billion, and in small it was $800 million.

A Rule of Thumb

These consensus closing levels ought to work as a good rule of thumb when you're considering investing in a fund. If you're looking at a fund with assets above these levels, you should be satisfied that it has greater capacity to handle the money. Look for low turnover because it will make the fund's asset base less taxing on trading costs. Look for a deep bench. Naturally, a company with lots of experienced managers and analysts, such as Wellington or American, is more capable of doing the additional legwork required than, say, a boutique shop with just a couple of investment professionals. You should also make sure you're getting a break on expenses. A large asset base should mean low expenses, which will at least partly compensate for the added problems of running large sums of money.

I should also mention that a new rule will make it easier to find out how big your fund really is. Fund companies often manage money in separate accounts using strategies similar to those employed at their funds. As a result, a fund's asset size actually understates the total amount under management. Soon, fund companies will have to disclose all the assets under management, and investors will have another club in their bag.

Etc.

One of the stranger news items from last week was a report that ING is planning a credit card to be used for loans against your 401(k). I can see the ad now:

Flat-screen plasma TV: $3,000
Vacation in Florida: $1,500
Knowing you've blown your retirement savings and will have to live off Social Security: Priceless.

Are the Hottest Funds of 2006 Worth Buying?

Fund Spy | By Russel Kinnel | 04-03-06 | 06:00 AM | This article originally appeared on Morningstar.com.

There's something particularly dangerous about lists of year-to-date fund returns when the year is still young. They capture such a short period of time, yet the returns of the leaders are always so darn enticing. Someone new to fund investing might think, "Why, if they just keep making that kind of return each quarter, I'll make a killing." Or perhaps they think that management has tapped into a growing trend, which is about to break wide open and make even more money. Unfortunately, such assumptions almost always end up costing investors money.

So, please, approach such lists warily. The top performers from the first quarter of 2006 are a case in point. Across the board, these funds have high costs and are extremely volatile, and some have lousy managers. Because of these traits, the odds are quite slim that if you bought one of these funds today you'd be happy with your decision 10 years from now.

Ten Funds Hot Enough to Burn

The kind of super-volatile, high-cost funds found in this quarter's top-10 list tend not to last long in investors' portfolios, or really at all. The fact is, a lot of these funds get killed off eventually. Alas, many trendy funds from years past—such as Steadman Oceanographic, Kinetics MidEast Peace, and Amerindo B2B—aren't around anymore.

Top-Performing Funds in 2006

Fund Name	YTD Return
Oberweis China Oppor (OBCHX)	36.64
U.S. Global Invest Wrld Prec Min (UNWPX)	34.50
Frontier MicroCap (FEFPX)	33.34
U.S. Global Investors Gold (USERX)	32.62
Dreyfus Premier Greater China (DPCAX)	29.38
Gartmore China Oppor (GOPIX)	27.10
ProFunds Ultra Small Cap (UAPIX)	26.89
Firsthand Technology Innov (TIFQX)	24.55
ProFunds Ultra Real Estate (REPIX)	24.00
Reynolds (REYFX)	23.97

Returns through 03-30-06.

Consider that only three of these 10 have a 10-year track record, and none of those three are appealing, despite their big first quarter. U.S. Global Investors World Precious Minerals has gained 4.99% on an annualized basis over the past 10 years, U.S. Global Investors Gold has a 4.89% annualized loss for the period, and Frontier MicroCap has posted an appalling 10-year annualized loss of 29.73%.

I'd bet that maybe one of the funds in this list will provide a nice return over the next 10 years, but even that one may produce poor results for its average shareholder because it's so hard to time these funds right. To make money in a highly volatile fund, you need to have the courage to buy when it is isn't hot (ideally when it's in the red) and then hold on through the horrifying losses.

Ten Funds Boring Enough to Depend On

I propose an alternative to the standard list of first-quarter winners. Instead of simply looking for the hottest short-term performance, I used Premium Fund Screener to create a list funds you'd actually want to own that also boast truly impressive performance.

First, I screened for funds that charge less than 1%, have a standard deviation no greater than that of Vanguard 500 Index (VFINX), and carry Stewardship Grades of B or better. Nothing profound here, I'm just looking for solid long-term performers that won't throw you with wild gyrations from quarter to quarter. Then I ranked the funds that passed my screen based on their performance relative to their category. The top funds are listed in the table below.

Solid Funds with Great Long-Term Performance

Fund	10-Year Cat Rank	10-Year Return
Mairs & Power Growth (MPGFX)	2	13.93
T. Rowe Price Capital Appreciation (PRWCX)	2	12.38
Vanguard Wellesley Income (VWINX)	2	8.75
American Century Equity Income (TWEIX)	3	12.61
Fidelity Balanced (FBALX)	6	11.06
Mairs & Power Balanced (MAPOX)	7	9.88
Jensen (JENSX)	9	9.88
T. Rowe Price Personal Strat Income (PRSIX)	10	8.05
American Funds American Balanced (ABALX)	11	9.87
Vanguard Wellington (VWELX)	11	10.01

Data through 02-28-06.

Most of the funds that made my alternative list own some bonds, which helps to reduce volatility. These funds are a bit boring, but they provide way better odds of making money—and sleeping better

doing it—than you could get by taking a flier on a
fund with scorching short-term returns.

The Only Muni-Fund Companies You Need

Fund Spy | By Russel Kinnel | 07-23-07 | 06:00 AM | This article originally appeared on Morningstar.com.

Choosing a municipal-bond fund can be a piece of cake—if you start by choosing the fund company before you look for the fund. Muni-bond funds are often team efforts, making the manager less important than the group behind the fund. Typically, a fund company will run all its muni funds with the same core philosophy and the same underlying fee structure. There's tremendous uniformity of quality and strategy within a fund company's muni operations.

It Gets Easier

Now I'm going to make it really easy by telling you to limit your search to just two fund companies (if you are a no-load investor). That's right, Fidelity and Vanguard are the only fund companies you need to know when you're looking for a tax-free bond fund. If you're familiar with the prowess of great bond firms such as BlackRock, PIMCO, and Western Asset, you may wonder why they aren't in the running. The reason is that they mostly manage money for giant institutions, such as pension funds, and pension funds don't need municipal bonds' tax advantages. (Click here to see all of our Fund Analyst Picks.) They have a couple of good muni funds here and there but it's just not where they focus their efforts.

That narrows the field to fund companies focused on individual investors. Although there are many worthy competitors, they don't measure up to Vanguard and Fidelity. Some muni funds run aggressive strategies, but most muni-bond investors are risk-averse types. Fidelity and Vanguard understand that. On the more cautious side, you can find solid choices at T. Rowe Price and American Century. But the funds cost a bit more, and their performance hasn't quite measured up. In addition, Vanguard now avoids bonds that may be vulnerable to the Alternative Minimum Tax, thus protecting you from tax risk. Fidelity Tax-Free Bond (FTABX) is AMT-free, but many of its other funds are not.

Vanguard has the lowest expense ratios among muni funds, and Fidelity is number two. Because of their big expense edge, both companies can avoid big risks and still deliver superior returns. In fact, they have built their strategies around that idea. Vanguard, in particular, plays it really close to the vest while trying to add value.

Fidelity's muni group avoids interest-rate bets by keeping a fund's duration (a measure of interest-rate sensitivity) in line with its benchmark. But managers try to add value by doing research to pick bonds that should modestly outperform similar issues. Do that enough times and it can add up to strong performance. In fact, Fidelity has the most impressive muni operation I've seen. It has great quantitative analysts who tease out inefficiencies to add value while stress-testing various scenarios to ensure that portfolios are well protected against any risks. In addition, Fidelity has good traders and issue-pickers. Put it together, and Fidelity is capable of making up a handicap of 0.2 to 0.3 percentage point on expense ratios it typically faces versus Vanguard.

The proof is in the performance. Both Vanguard's and Fidelity's muni funds excel. Of the 30 no-load muni funds between the two firms, 29 have returned better than their category averages over the trailing five years to May 1. Overall, Fidelity's muni funds are in the top 17% over the past five years and Vanguard's are in the top 21%.

Just a Few Decisions

To my mind, it's a coin flip. If you already have an account with one of the companies, stay there. All you have to do is decide whether you want to invest in a state or national fund (if your state has a high income tax, the answer is state) and whether to choose a fund that emphasizes long-term, intermediate-term, or short-term duration.

Sometimes mutual fund investing is hard, and sometimes it ain't.

Grantham Sees Huge Opportunity in "Anti-Risk"

Fund Spy | By Russel Kinnel | 07-30-07 | 06:00 AM | This article originally appeared on Morningstar.com.

Will a financial bubble crush small caps and hedge funds?

Jeremy Grantham says he's spotted the third great investing opportunity of his career. The first was small caps in the 1970s. The second was real estate, Treasury Inflation-Protected Securities, and value stocks during the tech bubble in 2000. Before you get too excited, I should make clear that the main opportunity today, in Grantham's view, is getting out of the way and watching the markets plummet in what he calls a slow-motion train wreck. Grantham made this call in a report published July 25—a day before the Dow got 300 points sliced off the top (talk about instant gratification!).

Grantham's firm, GMO, runs mostly institutional mutual funds but also runs half of Vanguard U.S. Value VUVLX and all of Evergreen Asset Allocation EAAFX. Grantham has always had a bearish tilt, so I typically take his warnings with a grain of salt. Still, he has been very much on the money with his warnings about the S&P 500 in 2000 and recommendations of foreign small caps, emerging markets, and timber.

In Grantham's view, we are in a financial-debt-soaked bubble that he's labeled the Blackstone Peak. Real estate and bonds are wobbly, and equities may weaken in October 2008. Grantham is a big believer in election cycles, which essentially means that the government floods the economy with money to get itself re-elected and then the market has a big hangover the following year when the bill comes due.

Grantham says that the excesses of private equity, hedge funds, and subprime debt mean lots of the economy and markets are leveraged to the gills and the end won't be pretty. He posits that in five years half the hedge funds will be out of business and one major bank will go belly-up. The first call isn't really that bold when you consider the survivorship rates of hedge funds, but the second is a whopper. I asked him about that, and he explained that he expects big banks to get burned by loaning money to private equity for a low return. He figures they'll get stuck with a few of those loans and take a bath. Moreover, he points out that most financial crises take down at least one big player.

Grantham calls this new opportunity "anti-risk." He says the opportunity lies more in bonds than stocks. "The ideal way of playing this third great opportunity is perhaps to create a basket of a dozen or more different anti-risk bets, for to speak the truth, none of us can know how this unprecedented risk bubble with its new levels of leverage and new instruments will precisely deflate. Some components, like subprime and junk bonds, may go early, and some equity risk spreads may go later."

Grantham's quarterly letter doesn't go into a lot of detail on what those dozen anti-risk bets should be, but he does express a love for TIPS. Given the substantial risk of inflation over the next 10 years, Grantham figures a yield of 2.4% to 2.6% on TIPS would make them attractive. "So, in recent weeks with TIPS selling between 2.6% and 2.8%, we have that rarest of rare birds, a genuinely cheap asset. Needless to say, where appropriate we have been grateful buyers."

Grantham also says he plans to sell his emerging-markets stocks near the end of the year.

I asked Grantham what else individual investors could do to make some anti-risk bets of their own. The wagers he's making for clients are too compli-cated for individuals, but he did offer a few ideas in addition to buying TIPS.

• Hold a lot of cash so that you'll have plenty of dry powder to take advantage of cheaper markets in years to come.

• Regular bonds are not too bad to own. (This means core high-quality bonds, such as corporate or Treasury bonds.)

• Short the Russell 2000 and go long on the S&P 500.

The final notion reflects Grantham's view that low-quality small caps will be terrible after many years of outperformance and high-quality large caps will fare well after years of lagging. The S&P 500 isn't a perfect proxy for GMO's definition of high qual-ity, but it's close. Grantham notes that 80% of the companies GMO considers high quality are in the United States. "If the economy weakens substan-tially, these stocks will be pure gold," he said. You can see the names GMO considers high quality in the portfolio of GMO U.S. Quality GQLOX. Unfor-tunately, you can't buy that fund unless your name is CalPERS.

Grantham's view that real estate and junk bonds are a bad place to be isn't unique. Quite a few savvy investors have sounded the warning on these apparently overheated asset classes. In fact, Morningstar's own REIT analysts have a dim view of their prospects. However, Grantham stands out in his predictions for the breadth and depth of the sell-off. In addition, I haven't heard a lot of people pounding the table for TIPS.

It's an interesting argument and Grantham, like most thoughtful bears, provides a valuable service in challenging bullish assumptions. Will I bail out on everything but TIPS? No, though I already have gotten out of my high-yield and real-estate funds for some of the same reasons spelled out above. In addition, I already have lots of blue-chip exposure. I might raise my TIPS weighting a percentage point or two, though.

In fact, GMO's funds aren't entirely bailing on mar-kets either, as they typically have tight constraints. The Evergreen Asset Allocation portfolio is instruc-tive. It's out of small caps but has plenty of expo-sure to core bonds and stocks as well as TIPS and emerging markets.

You can read all of Grantham's commentary and the firm's seven-year return outlook on GMO's Web site, though it requires a short registration form.

Big Real Estate Fund Launch Echoes Internet Fund Debacle

Fund Spy | By Russel Kinnel | 12-03-07 | 06:00 AM | This article originally appeared on Morningstar.com.

Amid the fallout of the 2000-02 bear market, one of the fund industry's biggest embarrassments was the slew of Internet funds launched just before the bubble burst. Big fund companies like Merrill Lynch and Strong and small shops like Amerindo, Turner, and Westcott launched funds that soon lost a lot of shareholders' money. Nearly all of those mistakes have been swept under the rug (that is, merged away or liquidated) but you can click here to see a few of the gems that came out.

In light of that debacle, many fund company executives vowed never to repeat that again. They recognized that their greed for assets blinded them to the need to do what's right for fundholders and that it's just plain wrong to launch a fund that you wouldn't touch.

Yet here we are, eight years later, and the fund industry has launched a truckload of real estate funds on unsuspecting and/or greedy investors. All told, 37 real estate funds have been launched this year (including those launched on the last day of 2006). The timing of those launches is just downright atrocious.

Consider some of the since-inception returns: IShares FTSE NAREIT Mortgage (REM) has lost 40% since inception, Ultra Real-Estate Proshares (EUR) is off 45%, and Cohen & Steers European Realty (EURAX) is down 27%.

REITs enjoyed a tremendous run from 2000 through 2006, to the point where it was pretty clear that they couldn't continue their pace. And while real estate funds typically buy commercial real estate securities, the mania in the housing market helped stoke investors' fervor for all things real estate. We saw rampant dot-com-style speculation in new homes, complete with two TV shows telling you how to flip a house. (Are they still on the air? If so, maybe they can tell people how to file for bankruptcy.)

So, most in the fund industry had to know that this year was a bad year to dive into real estate even before subprime joined the national lexicon. Plenty of real estate fund managers were telling us last year that REITs had become pretty unattractive, and we were also sounding cautionary notes. In September 2006, our John Coumarianos wrote: "Real estate is a good diversifier, but now's the time to trim, rather than add to, a position." Even in 2005, Christine Benz urged readers not to speculate in real estate and pointed to past severe corrections in residential real estate. In addition, stock analyst Craig Woker wrote a piece titled: "Real Estate Is the New Dot-Com: How to keep from getting burned in an overheated market." If we knew real estate was a bubble, you can be sure those launching funds knew it, too.

A fair number of the funds launched were global real estate funds, and I'll cut some slack on that count, given that REITs are fairly new overseas and it hadn't gotten as crazy overseas as here. But it's still a trendy launch, and the losses at Cohen & Steers Euro Realty illustrate that they have downside, too.

A new element in trendy fund launches is exchange-traded funds. They were still in their infancy for the dot-com boom, but they are in full swing today, and some can't resist any hot trend. Adelante has launched seven new real estate ETFs. Barclays has launched six new real estate iShares. The two firms are also at the forefront of carving out small niches in real estate that are reminiscent of the B2B funds launched in 2000. Adelante appears to have sliced real estate holdings by style so that there's growth, value, and yield. Barclays did subindustries such as residential and retail.

What's missing in this is that fund directors, managers, and executives aren't taking a step back to ponder their duty to fundholders. Should they launch something that they wouldn't touch? Are fundholders being served well when fund companies crank up marketing efforts after an extended run? Should we encourage investors to buy based on short-term performance?

If there's a silver lining here it's that many of the largest fund companies refrained from encouraging bubble investing. American, Vanguard, Fidelity, T. Rowe Price, AllianceBernstein, and Putnam are not on the list of those launching new real estate funds.

The Bloom Is Off 130/30 Funds

Fund Spy | By Russel Kinnel | 10-30-08 | 06:00 AM | This article originally appeared on Morningstar.com.

When 130/30 funds first came out, I was amused by the ideas I heard from reporters and a few investors that these funds would be good for choppy or down markets because they have long and short positions. True they do have shorts, I pointed out, but they're still 100% long whereas the typical equity fund is 95% long and 5% cash. It's an interesting idea, but don't look for a free lunch, was my response.

So, I'm not surprised that 130/30 funds as well as 120/20 funds are down like the rest of the world this year. But I am surprised by just how gosh darn bad they've been.

For background, 130/30 funds are funds that use leverage to have long positions equal to 130% of assets and shorts equal to 30%. The idea is that the manager is able to take advantage of research that indicates a stock is overpriced as well as stocks that are underpriced. Essentially you are leveraging up your bet on a manager's ability to add value though taking on only a bit more market risk than with a regular fund. The tricky part is that the manager has to be quite good at both longs and shorts to make it work.

And from the looks of it, not many managers have been able to add value in this strategy this year. Of the 18 leveraged net long (our phrase that encompasses 130/30 and 120/20 funds) funds only three are ahead of their category benchmark for the

year to date. Most are down much more than the S&P 500's 35% year-to-date loss. Consider RiverSource Contrarian Equity 120/20 (RCEAX) is down 46% and RiverSource 130/30 US Equity (RUSAX) is down 42%. RidgeWorth International Equity 130/30 (SCEIX) is down 58% or 800 basis points worse than MSCI EAFE thus showing 130/30 funds can do just as poorly overseas as here in the U.S. (RiverSource 130/30 U.S. Equity's managers just bolted for Putnam and the firm hasn't decided what's to become of the fund.)

Fidelity's new 130/30 Large Cap fund (FOTTX) is having a brutal start, too. It's down 29% in just three months which is about 600 basis points worse than the S&P 500.

What's Gone Wrong?

Having leverage and 100% net long exposure is a tough place to be in a bear market. Beyond that, it's clear that 130/30 managers are flailing around just like the rest of the managers. It would have been great if they'd had the insight to short the banks and other stocks that have been crushed and to go long on health care and the other stronger stocks, but that's not easy. Moreover, if I'm going to make a big bet on a manager's stock-selection skills, I'm going to pick one of the best with a proven record. There are some good managers running 130/30 funds but no real all-stars, which is why we don't have any 130/30 funds among our Fund Analyst Picks.

One Fund that Got It Right

There is one standout, though. MainStay 130/30 high yield (MYHAX) is down 16%. That's not pretty—but it's 1,000 basis points better than the index and beats nearly all high-yield funds. It's worth noting that MainStay's long-only portfolio has also outperformed though not quite as much as this one. Thus, it's not the magic of the 130/30 format, but rather managers making good calls that really matters. Managers Dan Roberts, Louis Cohen, Michael Kimble, and Taylor Wagenseil correctly saw that consumer discretionary issuers were especially vulnerable and instead invested in aerospace, energy, and specialty chemicals. They also shorted consumer dependent junk bonds from Nordstrom, Royal Caribbean, and Mexican home-builder Homex. That helped the 130/30 fund lose less than their long fund.

Also noteworthy is that they say the managers have been shorting bonds since the 1980s. You want that kind of expertise in a 130/30 fund be-cause shorting is different beast. Some 130/30 funds have those kinds of managers but at others I get the sense that it's kind of new.

Interestingly, they now have taken shorts down so that they are about 115/15. They say that with the high-yield market on its back the risk of shorts has increased and even some of the consumer depen-dent bonds look cheap now. In addition, they say hedge funds have piled into the short side because of the new restrictions on shorting stocks.

By the way, that success hasn't spread to Main-stay's 130/30 equity funds, all three of which lag their benchmark.

What's Next?

About 10 years ago, market-neutral funds were fresh and new. Many quickly proved to produce negative returns in any kind of market rather and they were quickly liquidated or merged away. I would imagine those 130/30 funds that are well behind their index have a rather brief time period in which to right the ship before being merged away.

More broadly, I doubt these funds will be able to draw much money (Mainstay's sole exception noted) now that it's clear there's no free lunch to be had.

What Mutual Funds We're Buying

Fund Spy | By Russel Kinnel | 11-24-08 | 06:00 AM | This article originally appeared on Morningstar.com.

What I'm Buying

With so many smart investors like Warren Buffett and Jeremy Grantham saying that stocks are cheap, I feel confident a lot of funds are going to prove to be good investments today even if we aren't at the bottom.

I've grouped my buy list into two types: stalwarts and rebound plays. The stalwarts have held up better than most, and the rebound plays have gotten smacked but have great managers who still know what they're doing. Which group you choose from should depend on whether your portfolio is full of financials-heavy, beaten-down funds like Clipper (CFIMX) and Weitz Value (WVALX) (go with the stalwarts) or funds that sidestepped the mess in favor of healthier companies (go with the rebound plays). For my own portfolio, I'm buying from both columns. I'm also imitating Jeremy Grantham by buying carefully and slowly. (Boosting your 401(k) contribution is one way.)

Stalwarts

Sequoia Fund (SEQUX), Jensen Fund (JENSX), Royce Special (RYSEX), Fairholme (FAIRX), Vanguard Primecap Core (VPCCX), Allianz NFJ Small Cap Value (PSVIX), Artisan International Value (ARTKX), and Harbor Bond (HABDX) have done brilliant jobs steering through the bear market. The stock funds have generally owned companies with little debt, which makes them far less dependent on wobbly banks. They are run by great stock-

pickers whom I trust to find great bargains amid the meltdown.

Rebound Plays

If you own these funds you might be too mad to send them more money. They underestimated the severity of the financial debacle and got burned. Yet, these are all funds that have made money for their investors over the long haul, have protected against losses in other bear markets, and still have the people and strategy in place that have worked well over a long time period. No fund or strategy is risk-free.

These are funds that might come roaring back when financials get off the mat. My rebound bets are Longleaf Partners (LLPFX), Selected American (SLADX), Dodge & Cox Stock (DODGX), Dodge & Cox International Stock (DODFX), and Loomis Sayles Bond (LSBRX).

For Selected and Dodge, the problem has been financials. Longleaf has a lot of economically sensitive stocks. Loomis Sayles Bond's problem has been corporate debt. Dan Fuss has been buying investment-grade and junk bonds at a time when everyone is fleeing to Treasuries. Treasuries are likely to offer poor returns in the future.

So far, I've added two new funds to my portfolio this fall: Jensen and Allianz NFJ Small Cap Value. Jensen has great high-quality names that will ride out this storm. Whenever great companies get cheap, it's a good idea to buy. Allianz NFJ Small Cap Value owns a fair number of financials, but they're the ones that stayed sober while others got drunk on leverage and derivatives. I'm also adding to positions in Selected American and Primecap Odyssey Aggressive Growth (POAGX).

Don Phillips: Buying Sequoia and Longleaf

Morningstar managing director Don Phillips has been buying muni funds and stock funds alike over the past 18 months. He reports that he's been buying Vanguard muni funds and Sequoia, Longleaf Partners, Dodge & Cox Stock, Baron Partners, and Fairholme. In addition, he bought Vanguard Inflation Protected Securities (VIPSX) and Vanguard Market Neutral.

Dan Culloton: Buying Vanguard Dividend Growth and Clipper

Meantime, our resident Vanguard expert is buying Vanguard Dividend Growth (VDIGX) and Clipper which he views as complementary. He likes the low-cost play on dividends as well as subadvisor Wellington's stock-selection skills.

"A lot of 'dividend growth' funds stretch the notion of growing dividends to stocks that have a lot of cash and earnings, but no record nor intention of paying a dividend," Dan says. "This one doesn't. I also like the dividend growth strategy; I think it's a good way find steady, profitable companies with redoubtable competitive advantages and decent long-term growth prospects. It helps that a Wellington manager who knows his limitations is at the helm. It has been light on financials because manager Don Kilbride has been suspicious of their dividend growth prospects for a couple of years (prior to the crisis payout ratios and ROEs were at all time highs)."

As for Clipper, Culloton notes Davis and Feinberg's outstanding record and their commitment of $5 million of their own money to the fund.

John Coumarianos: Buying Greenspring Fund

John Coumarianos has been buying Greenspring Fund (GRSPX) in part because it owns a slug of convertible bonds which have gotten very cheap lately. Convertibles have been pounded because some have credit risk but also because hedge funds love converts and have been forced to liquidate big positions in converts as investors pull their money out.

Ryan Leggio: Buying Jensen Fund

Meanwhile, Ryan Leggio is buying Jensen Fund. He likes its portfolio of high-quality wide-moat businesses. He also likes the fact that he can buy in when the market is trading below Jeremy Grantham's estimate of fair value.

Mike Breen: Buying Longleaf Partners Fund

Mike Breen is a contrarian value investor. So, when one of his longtime favorite funds is having a rough year, Breen is eager for the chance to buy its portfolio on the cheap. Longleaf's managers have said that stocks look particularly cheap this year. True, it's been an awful year, but the fund's long-term record is brilliant.

Appendix B

Vital Statistics on the 20 Funds That Passed Our Test

IN CHAPTER 10, I shared with you 20 outstanding funds that earned passing grades on all our tests. To shed some more light on those funds, here are some key data. We have fees, management info, and past performance through October 31, 2008. The relative rankings provided show how they've done relative to their category. They go from 100 (worst) to 1 (best). You can also look for fresh data on these funds at www.morningstar.com.

20 Funds That Passed: Fees

Fund Name	Expense Ratio	Front Load
Amer Funds CplncBldr A CAIBX	0.56	5.75
Amer Funds Fundamen A ANCFX	0.58	5.75
Columbia Acorn Intl Z ACINX	0.91	0.00
Dodge & Cox Balanced DODBX	0.53	0.00
Dodge & Cox Intl Stock DODFX	0.65	0.00
Fidelity Municipal Income FHIGX	0.47	0.00
Fidelity Spar Tot Mkt Inv FSTMX	0.10	0.00
FPA Capital FPPTX	0.88	5.25
Harbor Bond Instl HABDX	0.57	0.00
Janus Mid Cap Val Inv JMCVX	0.87	0.00
Matthews Pacific Tiger MAPTX	1.10	0.00
T. Rowe Price Eq Inc PRFDX	0.67	0.00
T. Rowe Price New Amer PRWAX	0.86	0.00
T. Rowe Price Sm Val PRSVX	0.82	0.00
TCW Total Return Bond I TGLMX	0.44	0.00
Vanguard Infl-Prot Secs VIPSX	0.20	0.00
Vanguard Intl Value VTRIX	0.43	0.00
Vanguard PRIMECAP Core VPCCX	0.55	0.00
Vanguard Total Bd Idx VBMFX	0.19	0.00
Vanguard Wellington VWELX	0.27	0.00

Data through October 31, 2008.

20 Funds That Passed: Management

Fund Name	Category	Stewardship Grade	Ownership Range ($)	Manager	Manager Tenure
Amer Funds CplncBldr A CAIBX	IH	B	1,000,000	Gordon, et al	16.90
Amer Funds Fundamen A ANCFX	LB	B	1,000,000	Kerr, et al	24.30
Columbia Acorn Intl Z ACINX	FR	B	500,000–1,000,000	Egan, et al	5.50
Dodge & Cox Balanced DODBX	MA	A	1,000,000	Lambert, et al	31.90
Dodge & Cox Intl Stock DODFX	LV	A	1,000,000	Kuo, et al	7.50
Fidelity Municipal Income FHIGX	ML	B	N/A	Thompson	6.40
Fidelity Spar Tot Mkt Inv FSTMX	LB	C	10,000–50,000	Adams, et al	3.70
FPA Capital FPPTX	MV	A	1,000,000	Rodriguez, et al	24.40
Harbor Bond Instl HABDX	GI	—	N/A	Gross	20.90
Janus Mid Cap Val Inv JMCVXa	MV	—	1,000,000	Perkins, et al	10.20
Matthews Pacific Tiger MAPTX	PJ	—	100,000–500,000	Shroff, et al	12.20
T. Rowe Price Eq Inc PRFDX	LV	—	1,000,000	Rogers	23.00
T. Rowe Price New Amer PRWAX	LG	—	750,000	Milano	6.30
T. Rowe Price Sm Val PRSVX	SB	A	1,000,000	Athey	17.20
TCW Total Return Bond I TGLMX	GI	—	1,000,000	Barach, et al	15.40
Vanguard Infl-Prot Secs VIPSX	IP	—	100,000–500,000	Volpert, et al	8.40
Vanguard Intl Value VTRIX	FV	B	N/A	Simms, et al	7.90
Vanguard PRIMECAP Core VPCCX	LG	A	1,000,000	Fried, et al	3.90
Vanguard Total Bd Idx VBMFX	GI	B	10,000–50,000	Volpert, et al	15.90
Vanguard Wellington VWELX	MA	A	1,000,000	Keogh, et al	5.90

Data through October 31, 2008.

Fund Categories

BL	Bank Loan Bond	**IB**	World Bond	**MY**	Muni New York Long
CA	Conservative Allocation	**IH**	World Allocation	**PJ**	Pacific ex-Japan Stock
CI	Intermediate-Term Bond	**IP**	Inflation Protected Bond	**SB**	Small-Cap Blend
CL	Long-Term Bond	**JS**	Japan Stock	**SC**	Speciality-Communications
CS	Short-Term Bond	**LB**	Large-Cap Blend	**SF**	Speciality-Financials
CV	Convertible Bond	**LG**	Large-Cap Growth	**SG**	Small-Cap Growth
DP	Diversified Pacific Stock	**IO**	Long-Short	**SH**	Specialty-Health
EB	Emerging Markets Bond	**LS**	Latin America Stock	**SI**	Muni Single-State Interm
EM	Diversified Emerging Markets	**LV**	Large-Cap Value	**SL**	Muni Single-State Long
ES	Europe Stock	**MA**	Moderate Allocation	**SP**	Specialty-Precious Metals
FA	Foreign Small/Mid Value	**MB**	Mid-Cap Blend	**SN**	Specialty-Natural Resources
FB	Foreign Large Blend	**MC**	Muni California Long	**SR**	Specialty-Real Estate
FG	Foreign Large Growth	**MF**	Muni California Int/Sh	**ST**	Specialty-Technology
FR	Foreign Small/Mid Growth	**MG**	Mid-Cap Growth	**SU**	Specialty-Utilities
FV	Foreign Large Value	**MI**	Muni National, Intermediate-Term	**SV**	Small-Cap Value
GI	Intermediate-Term Government Bond	**ML**	Muni National, Long-Term	**TA**	Target-Date 2000-2014
GL	Long-Term Government Bond	**MN**	Muni New York Int/Sh	**TB**	Target-Date 2015-2029
GS	Short-Term Government Bond	**MS**	Muni National, Short-Term	**TC**	Target-Date 2030+
HM	High-Yield Muni	**MU**	Multisector Bond	**UB**	Ultrashort Bond
HY	High-Yield Bond	**MV**	Mid-Cap Value	**WS**	World Stock

20 Funds That Passed: Performance

Fund Name	Annualized 10-Yr Total Return	% 10-Yr Category Rank	Annualized 15-Yr Total Return	% 15-Yr Category Rank
Amer Funds CpIncBldr A CAIBX	5.48	40	8.20	38
Amer Funds Fundamen A ANCFX	4.45	8	8.55	6
Columbia Acorn Intl Z ACINX	7.48	44	7.56	1
Dodge & Cox Balanced DODBX	5.42	5	8.01	10
Dodge & Cox Intl Stock DODFX	—	—	—	—
Fidelity Municipal Income FHIGX	4.15	1	4.66	7
Fidelity Spar Tot Mkt Inv FSTMX	1.19	35	—	—
FPA Capital FPPTX	7.96	16	11.34	1
Harbor Bond Instl HABDX	5.49	3	6.15	3
Janus Mid Cap Val Inv JMCVX	11.36	4	—	—
Matthews Pacific Tiger MAPTX	13.18	7	—	—
T. Rowe Price Eq Inc PRFDX	3.29	24	7.94	18
T. Rowe Price New Amer PRWAX	-0.67	54	4.14	73
T. Rowe Price Sm Val PRSVX	9.91	9	10.50	8
TCW Total Return Bond I TGLMX	5.83	1	6.31	2
Vanguard Infl-Prot Secs VIPSX	—	—	—	—
Vanguard Intl Value VTRIX	4.11	47	4.94	52
Vanguard PRIMECAP Core VPCCX	—	—	—	—
Vanguard Total Bd Idx VBMFX	4.74	13	5.46	11
Vanguard Wellington VWELX	4.63	9	8.23	7

Data through October 31, 2008.

Glossary

12b-1 fee

Maximum annual charge deducted from fund assets to pay for distribution and marketing costs.

administration fee

The amount that the fund spent on administration costs during the last fiscal year, as reported in the most recent annual report. This includes occupancy costs, office equipment, and fees for the administrator. If the fund has multiple share classes, the amount shown is prorated for that share class.

alpha

Also called Jensen's alpha, alpha is a systematic risk-adjusted return measure. It is the average difference between the excess return (total return minus the risk-free return) on a fund and the excess return on a benchmark multiplied by the systematic risk of the fund with respect to that benchmark (beta). It measures how much, on average, the fund added to (or subtracted from) the returns that could have been obtained from a position in the benchmark, levered or delevered so as to have the same beta as the fund. Alpha is measured as the intercept of the regression of the excess return on the fund as the dependent variable and the excess return on the benchmark as the independent variable. See *beta*.

automatic investment plan

An arrangement by which investors may initiate an account with a fund with a very small investment up-front, under the condition that they agree to invest a fixed amount per month in the future.

average market capitalization

The average market capitalization of a fund's equity portfolio gives you a measure of the size of the companies in which the fund invests.

Market capitalization is calculated by multiplying the number of a company's shares outstanding by its price per share.

At Morningstar we calculate this figure by taking the geometric mean of the market capitalizations of the stocks a fund owns.

beta

Beta is a measure of systematic risk with respect to a benchmark. Systematic risk is the tendency of the value of the fund and the value of benchmark to move together. Beta measures the sensitivity of the fund's excess return (total return minus the risk-free return) with respect to the benchmark's excess return that results from their systematic co-movement. It is the ratio of what the excess return of the fund would be to the excess return of the benchmark if there were no fund-specific sources of return. If beta is greater than 1, movements in value of the fund that are associated with movements in the value of the benchmark tend to be amplified. If beta is 1, they tend to be the same, and if beta is less than 1, they tend to be damped. If such movements tend to be in opposite directions, beta is negative. Beta is measured as the slope of the regression of the excess return on the fund as the dependent variable and the excess return on the benchmark as the independent variable.

breakpoint

The investment amount at which investors in a load fund qualify for a discount on the fund's sales charges.

category

In an effort to distinguish funds by what they own, as well as by their prospectus objectives and styles, Morningstar developed the Morningstar categories. While the prospectus objective identifies a fund's investment goals based on the wording in the fund prospectus, the Morningstar category identifies funds based on their actual investment styles as measured by their underlying portfolio holdings.

closed fund

An open-end fund that has, either temporarily or permanently, stopped taking new investors. This usually occurs when management finds the fund's increasing asset size to be disadvantageous.

duration

A time measure of a bond's interest-rate sensitivity, based on the weighted average of the time periods over which a bond's cash flows accrue to the bondholder. Time periods are weighted by multiplying by the present value of its cash flow divided by the bond's price. (A bond's cash flows consist of coupon payments and repayment of capital). A bond's duration will almost always be shorter than its maturity, with the exception of zero-coupon bonds, for which maturity and duration are equal.

expense projections (3-, 5-, and 10-year)

The SEC mandates that each fund list its expense projections. Found in the fund's prospectus, these figures show how much an investor would expect to pay in expenses sales charges (loads) and fees over the next three, five, and 10 years, assuming a $10,000 investment that grows by 5 percent per year, with redemption at the end of each time period. Expense projections are commonly based on the past year's incurred fees or an estimate of the current fiscal year's fees, should a portion of the overall fee structure change as of the printing of the fund's most current prospectus. Newer funds are required to print expense projections for only one- and three-year time periods because longer-term projections may not be possible to estimate.

fee waiver

The elimination of all or part of a fund's expenses and fees. Funds, particularly fixed-income funds, adopt this practice at various times to make their returns more competitive.

high-yield bonds

A bond rated Ba or lower by Moody's or BB or lower by Standard & Poor's, or an unrated bond.

index fund

A fund that tracks a particular index and attempts to match returns. While an index typically has a much larger portfolio than a mutual fund, the fund's management may study the index's movements to develop a representative sampling, and match sectors proportionately.

load

Load denotes either a fund's maximum initial or deferred sales charge. For initial (front-end) loads, this figure is expressed as a percentage of the initial investment and is incurred upon purchase of fund shares. For deferred sales charges, the amount charged is based on the lesser of the initial or final value of the shares sold.

management fee

The management fee is the maximum percentage deducted from a fund's average net assets to pay an advisor or subadvisor. Often, as the fund's net assets grow, the percentage deducted for management fees decreases. Alternatively, the fund may compute the fee as a flat percentage of average net assets. A portion of the management fee may also be charged in the form of a group fee. To determine the group fee, the fund family creates a sliding scale for the family's total net assets and determines a percentage applied to each fund's asset base. The management fee might also be amended by or be primarily composed of a performance fee, which raises or lowers the management fee based on the fund's returns relative to an established index (we list the maximum by which the fee can increase or decrease). It might also be composed of a gross income fee—a percentage based on the total amount of income generated by the investment portfolio. The administrative fee is the fund's maximum.

Morningstar risk

An annualized measure of a fund's downside volatility over a 3-, 5-, or 10-year period. This is a component of the Morningstar risk-adjusted return.

Morningstar risk-adjusted ratings

Often simply called the Star rating, the Morningstar rating brings load-adjustments, performance (returns), and risk together into one evaluation. To determine a fund's star rating for a given time period (3, 5, or 10 years), the fund's risk-adjusted return is plotted on a bell curve: If the fund scores in the top 10 percent of its category, it receives five stars (highest); if it falls in the next 22.5 percent, it receives four stars (above average); a place in the middle 35 percent earns three stars (average); those lower still, in the next 22.5 percent, receive two stars (below average); and the bottom 10 percent get only one star (lowest). The overall Morningstar rating is a weighted average of the available 3-, 5-, and 10-year ratings.

Morningstar risk-adjusted return

MRAR is an enhanced measure of a fund's performance and risk. It is based on expected utility theory, which recognizes that investors are (a) more concerned about a possible poor outcome than an unexpectedly good outcome and (b) willing to give up some portion of their expected return in exchange for greater certainty of return. The risk-adjusted return accounts for all variations in a fund's month-to-month performance, with more emphasis on downward risk. This rewards consistent performance and reduces the possibility that strong short-term performance will mask the inherent risk of a fund.

MPT statistics (modern portfolio theory)

Alpha, beta, and R-squared are modern-portfolio-theory measures of a fund's relative risk, based on a least-squares regression of a fund's excess returns on the excess returns of a market index.

net assets

The month-end net assets of the mutual fund, recorded in millions of dollars. Net-asset figures are useful in gauging a fund's size, agility, and popularity. They help determine whether a small company fund, for example, can remain in its investment-objective category if its asset base reaches an ungainly size.

net asset value

Net asset value tells you what each share is worth, but don't read too much into it. Some people treat it like a stock price or a stock P/E and target buy points at certain levels for a fund. But in fact, that strategy doesn't make a whole lot of sense. NAV is not the same as total returns—a fund could pay a big dividend and that would drop its NAV, yet it would not have any impact on the fund's return or the value of your investment.

no-load fund

Any fund with no front load, no deferred load, and 12b-1 fees less than or equal to 0.25 percent. Management fees, however, may be higher, because marketing charges come directly out of pocket. True no-load funds are normally, but not always, cheaper to own than load funds with distribution fees. While true no-load funds may be attractive from an expense standpoint, this does not suggest that funds with loads should be shunned. Many funds with consistently above-average track records have fees and expenses attached. In many cases, these may be marketing fees (often 12b-1 fees) or charges to cover administrative costs, rather than broker commissions.

P/E ratio (price to earnings), current

A stock's current price divided by the company's trailing 12-month earnings per share.

percentile rank in category

Percentile rank is a standardized way of ranking items within a peer group, in this case, funds with the same Morningstar category. The observation with the largest numerical value is ranked 1; the observation with the smallest numerical value is ranked 100. The remaining observations are placed equal distance from one another on the rating scale. Note that lower percentile ranks are generally more favorable for returns (high returns), while higher percentile ranks are generally more favorable for risk measures (low risk).

redemption fee

The redemption fee is an amount charged when money is withdrawn from the fund. This fee does not go back into the pockets of the fund company, but rather into the fund itself, and thus does not represent a net cost to shareholders. Also, unlike contingent deferred sales charges, redemption fees typically operate only in short, specific time clauses, commonly

30, 180, or 365 days. However, some redemption fees exist for up to five years. These fees are typically imposed to discourage market-timers, whose quick movements into and out of funds can be disruptive.

return after taxes

Return after taxes shows a fund's annualized tax-adjusted and load-adjusted total return for the time period specified. Interest income, dividends, and capital gains are each taxed at the highest federal tax rate prevailing. State and local taxes as well as individual-specific issues are ignored. (*Note:* Most interest income from municipal-bond funds is exempt from federal tax, while capital gains from municipal bond funds are taxable.)

Per the SEC's guidance about this topic, all aftertax returns are also adjusted for loads and recurring fees. Therefore, these are technically "load- and tax-adjusted returns" and not simply "tax-adjusted returns." Therefore, a fund's aftertax return may be lower than its total return because of tax reasons, sales charges, or both.

For investments in taxable accounts, taxes are often a big factor in the economic benefits an investor realizes. Aftertax returns are thus a very useful way of comparing one fund to another. For taxable accounts, tax-efficient funds (those that make small income and capital gains distributions) should be heavily favored over tax-inefficient funds.

R-squared

A measure of the goodness-of-fit of a regression. R-squared is always between 0 (no fit) and +1 (perfect fit). In a regression with only one independent variable, such as that used to estimate alpha and beta, R-squared is the square of the correlation between the dependent and independent variable.

Sharpe ratio

A risk-adjusted measure developed by Nobel Laureate William Sharpe, the Sharpe ratio is calculated by using standard deviation and excess return to determine reward per unit of risk. The higher the Sharpe ratio, the better the fund's historical risk-adjusted performance. The Sharpe ratio is calculated for the past 36-month period by dividing a fund's annualized excess returns by the standard deviation of a fund's annualized excess returns. Because this ratio uses standard deviation as its risk measure, it is most appropriately applied when analyzing a fund that is an investor's sole holding. The Sharpe ratio can be used to compare two funds directly on how much risk a fund had to bear to earn excess return over the risk-free rate.

standard deviation

A statistical measurement of dispersion about an average, which, for a mutual fund, depicts how widely the returns varied over a certain period of time. Investors use the standard deviation of historical performance to try to predict the range of returns that are most likely for a given fund. When a fund has a high standard deviation, the predicted range of performance is wide, implying greater volatility. Standard deviation is most appropriate for measuring risk if it is for a fund that is an investor's only holding. The figure cannot be combined for more than one fund because the standard deviation for a portfolio of multiple funds is a function of not only the individual standard deviations, but also of the degree of correlation among the funds' returns. If a fund's returns follow a normal distribution, then approximately 68 percent of the time they will fall within one standard deviation of the mean return for the fund, and 95 percent of the time within two standard deviations. Morningstar computes standard deviation using the trailing monthly total returns for the appropriate time period. All of the monthly standard deviations are then annualized.

Style Box

The Morningstar Style Box™ was introduced in 1992 to help investors and advisors determine the investment style of a fund. The equity Style

Box is a nine-square grid that classifies securities by size along the vertical axis and by value and growth characteristics along the horizontal axis. Different investment styles often have different levels of risk and lead to differences in returns. Therefore, it is crucial that investors understand style and have a tool to measure their style exposure. In general, a growth-oriented portfolio will hold the stocks of companies that the portfolio manager believes will increase factors such as sales and earnings faster than the rest of the market. A value-oriented portfolio contains mostly stocks the manager thinks are currently undervalued in price and will eventually see their worth recognized by the market. A blend portfolio might be a mix of growth stocks and value stocks, or it may contain stocks that exhibit both characteristics. The Morningstar Style Box helps investors construct diversified, style-controlled portfolios based on the style characteristics of all the stocks and funds included in that portfolio.

The Morningstar Style Box captures three of the major considerations in equity investing: size, security valuation, and security growth. Value and growth are measured separately because they are distinct concepts. A stock's value orientation reflects the price that investors are willing to pay for some combination of the stock's anticipated per-share earnings, book value, revenues, cash flow, and dividends. A high price relative to these measures indicates that a stock's value orientation is weak, but it does not necessarily mean that the stock is growth-oriented. Instead, a stock's growth orientation is independent of its price and reflects the growth rates of fundamental variables such as earnings, book value, revenues, and cash flow. When neither value nor growth is dominant, stocks are classified as "core" and portfolios are classified as "blend."

tax cost ratio

The tax cost ratio for a fund is a comparison of pretax and aftertax returns. It is the percent of assets that an investor loses to taxes. Investors can use this data point to determine how effectively the fund manager manages tax issues or to compare one fund to another.

total return

This is a sum of appreciation and income. It assumes that dividends are reinvested. Essentially, this is the fund's bottom line. The figure usually does not reflect a sales load but does come after expenses are deducted.

total return, annualized

Returns for periods longer than one year are expressed as annualized returns. This is equivalent to the compound rate of return, which, over a certain period of time, would produce a fund's total return over that same period.

turnover ratio

This is a measure of the fund's trading activity that is computed by taking the lesser of purchases or sales (excluding all securities with maturities of less than one year) and dividing by average monthly net assets. A turnover ratio of 100 percent or more does not necessarily suggest that all securities in the portfolio have been traded. In practical terms, the resulting percentage loosely represents the percentage of the portfolio's holdings that have changed over the past year.

About the Author

Russel Kinnel is director of mutual fund research for Morningstar, and editor of *Morningstar FundInvestor*, a monthly print newsletter for individual investors.

He also oversees Morningstar's Fund Analyst Picks, which represent the analysts' ideas of top funds on a category-by-category basis, and Morningstar's Fund Analyst Pans, which is a list of funds the analysts recommend investors avoid. He also writes the "Fund Spy" column for Morningstar. com, the company's Web site for individual investors.

Kinnel joined the company in 1994. He holds a bachelor's degree in economics and journalism from the University of Wisconsin, Madison.

Index